A-Z OF
FAVORITE FRUITS

A~Z OF
FAVORITE FRUITS

ARCO PUBLISHING, INC.
New York

Published 1985 by Arco Publishing, Inc.
215 Park Avenue South, New York, NY 10003

© Marshall Cavendish Limited 1985

Library of Congress Cataloging in Publication Data
Main entry under title:

A-Z of favorite fruits.

  Includes index.
  1. Cookery (Fruit)   I. Arco Publishing.   II. Title:
A to Z of favorite fruits.
TX811.A2   1985   641.6′4   84-16863
ISBN 0-668-06328-9
ISBN 0-668-06332-7 (pbk.)

Printed and bound in Hong Kong by
Dai Nippon Printing Company

Cook's Notes

The handy hints you've always wanted to know.

TIME
Timing explained –
black symbol means
allow extra time

FREEZING
The essential guide to
dishes which freeze

ECONOMY
Tips to make dishes go
further, or for inexpen-
sive ingredients

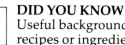
WATCHPOINT
Look out for special
advice on tricky methods

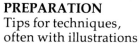
DID YOU KNOW
Useful background to
recipes or ingredients

PREPARATION
Tips for techniques,
often with illustrations

SERVING IDEAS
Suggestions for good
accompaniments

**SPECIAL
OCCASIONS**
Ideas to lift a dish
out of the ordinary

VARIATIONS
Interesting ways to alter
the basic dish

COOK'S TIPS
Background
information to help
when you need it

BUYING GUIDE
Guide to selecting
suitable ingredients

PRESSURE COOKING
How to save time with
your pressure cooker

FOR CHILDREN
Adapting dishes
for children's tastes

STORAGE
How to store and for
how long

INTRODUCTION

Whether you feel like sampling the crunch of a crisp green apple or the smoothness of a luscious ripe peach, the A-Z OF FAVORITE FRUITS brings you a dish to suit your mood. Recipes range from fabulous desserts to crisp tasty salads and unusual main courses; there are quick and easy ideas for instant meals, as well as more elaborate dishes for entertaining. Not only do we show you how to make the most of the full flavor of fresh fruit, but also give you new creative ways with 'convenient' canned fruit.

Arranged in an easy-to-follow alphabetical format, you can simply turn to the fruit you are interested in and try the recipes suggested. There is also a comprehensive index to help you find the perfect recipe to suit the occasion.

Each recipe is set out in a simple step-by-step style and is accompanied by Cook's Notes giving all sorts of handy hints, ranging from tips on preparation to serving ideas.

Apple and bacon pie

SERVES 4
2 green apples
½ lb basic pie dough, thawed if frozen
¾ lb smoked bacon, chopped
1 large onion, thinly sliced
2 potatoes, cut into ⅛ inch slices
freshly ground black pepper
¾ cup medium or dry cider
margarine, for greasing
milk, for brushing

1 Preheat the oven to 400°. Grease a 5-cup deep flameproof dish.
2 Roll out the dough on a floured surface to a shape slightly larger than the circumference of the dish. Cut off a long narrow strip of dough all around the edge. Reserve this and other trimmings.
3 Put the bacon, onion and potatoes in a bowl. Pare, core and slice the apples, then add to the bowl with plenty of pepper. Stir well to mix. Transfer the mixture to the greased dish, then pour over the cider.
4 Brush the rim of the dish with water, then press the narrow strip of dough all around the rim. Brush the strip with a little more water, then place the large piece of dough on top. Trim the edge of the dough, then raise up and flute.
5 Make leaves or other shapes with the dough trimmings, then place on top of the pie, brushing the underside with water so that they do not come off during baking. Make a small hole in the center of the pie for the steam to escape, then brush all over the dough with milk.
6 Bake in the oven for 20 minutes, then lower the heat to 350° ✳ and bake for a further 30-40 minutes ⚠ until the potatoes are tender when pierced with a fine skewer. Serve hot.

Cook's Notes

TIME
If using frozen dough, the pie will only take 10-15 minutes to prepare, but if making your own dough it will take about 30 minutes, plus an extra 30 minutes chilling Baking time for the pie is 50-60 minutes.

SERVING IDEAS
The pie may be served by itself, or with a light vegetable accompaniment such as baked tomatoes or buttered peas.

●700 calories per portion

FREEZING
Cook the pie in a foil container, but leave in oven for only 20 minutes after you have turned down the heat. Cool quickly, cover the top with foil, then wrap in a plastic bag. Seal, label and freeze for up to 2 months.

To serve: Thaw the pie overnight in the refrigerator, then reheat at 350° for about 30 minutes.

WATCHPOINT
If the dough begins to brown too quickly during baking, cover it with foil.

Apple mint jelly

MAKES ABOUT 1½ LB
2 lb tart apples, chopped
2 cups cider vinegar
2 cups water
2 cups sugar
3-4 tablespoons finely chopped
  fresh mint
¼ teaspoon green food coloring

1 Put the apples in a large heavy-bottomed pan together with the cider vinegar and water. Bring to a boil, then lower the heat slightly and simmer for 30-40 minutes, or until the apples are very soft and pulpy. Remove from heat.

2 Hang a damp jelly bag over a large bowl and pour the apple pulp into the bag. Leave to strain through overnight (see Cook's tip).

3 Transfer the strained juice to a large pan, add the sugar and heat gently, stirring, until the sugar has dissolved. Clip a candy thermometer, if you have one, onto the edge of the pan. Bring to a boil, then continue to fast boil for about 5 minutes until the thermometer reads 220°, or when a teaspoon of the jelly placed on a cold saucer wrinkles when a finger is pulled gently across the surface.

4 Remove the pan from the heat, leave on one side for 5 minutes, skim off any foam with a large spoon, then stir in the chopped fresh mint and green food coloring.

5 Pour the jelly immediately into clean, hot, sterilized jars and seal. Cool completely (see Storage).

Cook's Notes

TIME
35 minutes preparation; plus straining overnight; then about 15 minutes, plus cooling time.

COOK'S TIP
If you do not have a jelly bag, line a colander with several layers of scalded cheesecloth, so that the cheesecloth hangs over the edge. Set lined colander over a bowl so that the colander does not touch the base of the bowl. Pour the apple pulp into the lined colander and leave until the juice has dripped through.

VARIATION
Gooseberries make a delicious alternative to apples, and gooseberry jelly goes particularly well with all hot and cold cheese dishes. Omit the mint.

STORAGE
The jelly can be eaten at once; unopened, it can be kept for up to 6 months in a cool, dark place.

SERVING IDEAS
This is the perfect accompaniment to roast and cold lamb; it is also very good with cold roast pork.

● 50 calories per tablespoon

Apple and walnut crêpes

MAKES 12
1 cup all-purpose flour
pinch of salt
1 large egg, lightly beaten
2 tablespoons butter, melted
1¼ cups milk
butter, for greasing
cream or ice cream, to serve

FILLING AND GLAZE
2 lb tart apples
1 cup sugar
2 tablespoons water
finely grated rind of 1 lemon
2 tablespoons apricot jam
¼ cup chopped walnuts

1 Sift flour and salt into a bowl. Make a well in the center. Add egg, melted butter and 2 tablespoons milk. Beat together, then slowly beat in remaining milk.
2 Strain batter into a pitcher, cover and leave for 30 minutes.

3 Meanwhile, make the filling: Pare, core and slice the apples, then put into a saucepan with sugar and water. Cover and cook gently for 15-20 minutes until apples are very soft. Turn into a strainer to drain off excess liquid, then return apples to pan. Stir in lemon rind, cover and keep hot.
4 Preheat the oven to 350°.
5 Melt a little butter in a heavy-bottomed 6 inch skillet over moderate to high heat. Pour off any excess.
6 Beat the batter. Remove skillet from heat and pour in just enough batter to cover base thinly (see Cook's tip). Return to heat and cook crêpe for about 1 minute, until underside is set. Using a spatula, turn crêpe over and cook on the other side for 20-30 seconds. Lift crêpe onto waxed paper.
7 Continue making crêpes interleaving each with waxed paper, until there are 12 altogether. Stir batter frequently and grease pan with more butter as necessary.
8 Spread about 1 tablespoon apple filling over one-half of each crêpe.

Fold crêpes in half, then in quarters; arrange in a buttered ovenproof dish and heat through in the oven for 10 minutes.
9 Put jam into a small pan and heat until bubbling. Brush over crêpes, then sprinkle with walnuts. Serve at once, with cream.

Cook's Notes

TIME
Total preparation and cooking time, including time for the batter to rest, is about 1 hour.

COOK'S TIP
As soon as the batter touches the pan, tilt the pan around using a semi-circular action to spread the batter evenly. Use the first crêpe as a "tester" to judge the amount of batter needed and the temperature of the pan.

●200 calories per crêpe

Avocado and egg bake

SERVES 6
1 large avocado
6 eggs, separated
6 tablespoons browned bread crumbs (see Preparation)
3 tablespoons vegetable oil
1 onion, finely chopped
1 clove garlic, crushed (optional)
¼ cup finely chopped fresh parsley
salt and freshly ground black pepper
¾ cup shredded Cheddar cheese
melted margarine or butter, for greasing

1 Preheat the oven to 400°. Brush 6 individual ovenproof dishes with melted margarine, then coat them evenly with 4 tablespoons of the bread crumbs. Set the dishes aside.
2 Heat the oil in a skillet, add the onion and garlic, if using, and cook gently for 3-4 minutes until the onion is soft but not colored. Set the cooked onions aside to cool for about 5 minutes.
3 Cut the avocado in half. Remove the seed, scoop out the flesh into a bowl, then mash with a fork to a purée. Beat in the egg yolks and parsley, then the cooled onion and salt and pepper to taste.
4 Beat the egg whites until standing in stiff peaks, then fold them into the avocado mixture. Pile into the dishes, scatter remaining crumbs on top and bake in the oven for 20 minutes.
5 Sprinkle the top of the rising mixture with the cheese, then return dishes to the oven for a further 15 minutes until they are well risen and golden. Serve at once.

Cook's Notes

TIME
Preparation takes about 30 minutes, plus 30 minutes for making bread crumbs, cooking 35 minutes.

PREPARATION
To make the quantity of browned bread crumbs needed for this recipe: Toast 3-4 slices of day-old white bread in a 350° oven for 20 minutes until golden. Cool, then put in a plastic bag and crush with a rolling pin.

SERVING IDEAS
Serve with French bread and a salad.

●330 calories per portion

Banana and carrot salad

SERVES 4
4 bananas
2 large carrots
2 tablespoons golden raisins
8-12 lettuce leaves
sprigs of parsley, for garnish

DRESSING
⅓ cup sunflower oil
2 tablespoons lemon juice
1 teaspoon curry powder
pinch of dry mustard
pinch of sugar
salt and freshly ground black pepper

1 Make the dressing: Put all the dressing ingredients into a small bowl and beat with a fork until thoroughly combined. Season to taste with salt and pepper.

2 Finely grate the carrots, put into a bowl with the raisins and mix well. Pour two-thirds of the dressing over the carrot mixture and toss to coat well.

3 Arrange the lettuce leaves on 4 individual salad plates. Halve the bananas lengthwise ⚠ and lay 2 halves on each bed of lettuce.

4 Drizzle the remaining dressing over each banana half, then divide the carrot mixture between each plate, spooning the mixture between the banana halves.

5 Garnish each serving with sprigs of parsley and serve at once.

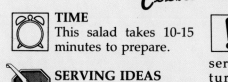

Cook's Notes

⏰ TIME
This salad takes 10-15 minutes to prepare.

🥄 SERVING IDEAS
The contrasting sweet and sharp flavors of this salad go well with cold sliced chicken or ham − serve as a light lunch or supper accompanied by wholewheat rolls or bread and butter. Alternatively, try serving the salad as an unusual appetizer.

⚠ WATCHPOINT
Do not peel and slice the bananas until just before serving, otherwise they will turn brown and look very unappetizing.

VARIATION
Garnish each serving with a sprinkling of roughly chopped walnuts for added crunchiness.

●280 calories per portion

Banana with ham fritters

SERVES 4
4 bananas
1 cup ground cooked ham
3 eggs, beaten
1 cup soft bread crumbs
⅔ cup milk
freshly ground black pepper
6 tablespoons butter
parsley sprigs, for garnish

1 In a bowl, beat together the ham, eggs and bread crumbs.
2 Put the milk in a small saucepan and bring to a boil. Stir the milk into the ham mixture. Season to taste with pepper and mix everything together thoroughly.
3 Melt 1 tablespoon butter in a large skillet over moderate heat. When the butter is hot and foaming, spoon tablespoonfuls of half the mixture into the pan. Cook for 1-2 minutes until well browned, then turn them over using a slotted spatula and cook for a further 1-2 minutes. Drain on kitchen paper and keep warm while you prepare the next batch.
4 Melt another tablespoon butter and cook the other half of the mixture in the same way. Drain on kitchen paper and keep warm in a very low oven.
5 Lower the heat under the pan and melt the remaining butter. Peel the bananas and cut each in half lengthwise. Cook gently in the butter for 3-4 minutes, shaking the pan so that the butter coats all the bananas thoroughly.
6 Arrange the fritters on a warmed serving dish and put the bananas around them. Garnish with sprigs of parsley.

Cook's Notes

TIME
The fritters take about 5 minutes to make and 8 minutes or so to cook.

SERVING IDEAS
As the fritters and bananas make a rather rich, filling meal, serve with something sharp-flavored as a contrast. A mixed green salad tossed in an oil and vinegar dressing would be ideal.

VARIATIONS
Use any cold left-over meat in these fritters. Add a few sautéed mushrooms, a grated small onion or ½ a green or sweet red pepper.

●280 calories per fritter

Banana pastry cakes

MAKES 16
4 large bananas
1 package (17¼ oz) puff pastry
1-2 tablespoons lemon juice
1 cup sugar
½ teaspoon ground cinnamon
¼ teaspoon grated nutmeg
¼ teaspoon ground cloves
1 egg beaten with 1 tablespoon water
confectioners' sugar

1 Preheat the oven to 425°. Unfold both sheets of pastry on a lightly floured working surface. Roll out to 20 × 10 inch rectangles, 〔!〕 trim, then cut into eight 5 inch squares.

2 Peel and slice bananas into 4 equal-size pieces. Brush each piece with lemon juice. Combine sugar, cinnamon, nutmeg and cloves in a small bowl, then roll the banana pieces in the spice mixture to coat.

3 Place 1 coated banana piece in center of a pastry square. Brush the edges of the pastry square with the beaten egg mixture, then fold over the pastry (see Preparation).

4 Brush the pastry cakes with the remaining beaten egg; sprinkle with remaining spice mixture. Place on ungreased baking sheets, spacing well. Bake 10 minutes. Lower the oven temperature to 350° and bake 8-10 minutes or until pastry is golden.

5 Cool on wire racks and sprinkle with confectioners' sugar.

Cook's Notes

TIME
Preparation time 30 minutes, cooking time 18-20 minutes.

PREPARATION
Roll up the spiced banana pastry cakes as shown below:

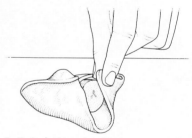

1 *Bring the 2 opposite corners of the pastry together across the length of the banana. Overlap the ends of the dough over the top of the banana and press firmly to seal.*

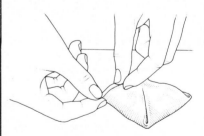

2 *Bring the other 2 corners to the center and overlap them on top of the first 2 corners. Press firmly to seal.*

3 *Fold over the open edges slightly and press to seal.*

! WATCHPOINT
Do not stretch pastry or it will shrink during baking. To prevent this, let the dough rest for 5-10 minutes after rolling out.

●170 calories each

Bananas in spiced orange sauce

SERVES 4
4 bananas
1 tablespoon sugar
¼ teaspoon apple pie spice
**finely grated rind and juice of
1 orange**
1 tablespoon butter

1 Mix the sugar and spice, then add to the orange rind and juice and stir well to blend. Cut the bananas diagonally across into chunky, slanting pieces.
2 Melt the butter in a heavy-bottomed saucepan. Add bananas and cook briskly for 2 minutes,

turning them with a slotted spatula ⚠ until evenly browned.
3 Stir the orange juice mixture, then pour over the bananas. Let the mixture bubble for a few seconds,

until heated through, ⚠ then remove the pan from the heat.
4 Spoon the hot bananas and orange sauce into 4 bowls and serve at once.

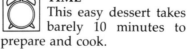

TIME
This easy dessert takes barely 10 minutes to prepare and cook.

⚠ WATCHPOINTS
Take care when turning the banana pieces not to break them or the finished dish will not look attractive.

Do not cook the sauce too long, or the bananas will become mushy.

SERVING IDEAS
For a more substantial dessert, spoon the bananas and sauce over chocolate or vanilla ice cream; decorate with thin strips of pared orange rind which have been blanched in boiling water for 2-3 minutes, then drained and refreshed under cold water and drained again.

●130 calories per portion

Blueberry softie

SERVES 6
1 can (about 10 oz) blueberries
finely grated rind of 1 orange
1¼ cups heavy cream
1 tablespoon Grand Marnier
**   liqueur**
2 egg whites
¼ cup sugar
strips of orange rind, to decorate
**   (optional)**
crisp, orange-flavored cookies, to
**   serve**

1 Sieve the blueberries and their juice into a bowl, or purée in a blender. Beat in the orange rind then pour into a freezerproof container. Cover and place in the freezer or freezer compartment of the refrigerator until half frozen (see Cook's tip).

2 Whip the cream with the liqueur until standing in soft peaks. In a clean bowl and with clean beaters, beat the egg whites until stiff, then beat in the sugar, 1 tablespoon at a time. Using a large metal spoon, fold the egg whites into the cream and liqueur mixture.

3 Turn the half-frozen purée into a bowl and mash it with a fork, then carefully fold in the cream mixture.

4 Spoon into chilled glasses and decorate with strips of orange rind, if liked. Top each portion with 2 cookies and serve at once.

Cook's Notes

TIME
Preparation takes 25 minutes but allow several hours for freezing.

COOK'S TIP
Turn the refrigerator down to its coldest setting 1 hour before you start the preparation. Use a shallow metal tray for freezing the blueberry purée. Remember to turn the refrigerator back to its normal setting when you have finished making the blueberry softie.

●295 calories per portion

Cherry dessert

SERVES 8
3 cans (about 16 oz) Bing cherries,
syrup drained and reserved
1¼ cups cream cheese
1¼ cups dairy sour cream
1 tablespoon arrowroot
2 tablespoons kirsch

1 Divide the cherries between 8 glass serving dishes.
2 Beat the fresh cream cheese until light, then beat in the sour cream until well mixed. Pour the mixture over the cherries.
3 Pour 1¼ cups of reserved syrup into a pan and bring to a boil. Mix the arrowroot with a little of the remaining syrup in a bowl and mix to a smooth paste.
4 Add the heated syrup to the arrowroot paste, stir thoroughly and return to the pan. Put the pan over gentle heat and stir until the syrup has thickened.
5 Remove pan from heat and stir in the kirsch. Let cool, then spoon onto each bowl. Cover and refrigerate for 2 hours.
6 Remove the bowls from the refrigerator and serve at once.

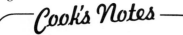

Cook's Notes

 TIME
This simple dessert takes 20 minutes to prepare, plus 2 hours chilling time.

SERVING IDEAS
For a crisp contrast, serve the dessert with a selection of small, crunchy cookies – wafers, macaroons and Scotch shortbread are ideal. Alternatively, serve with small meringues.

DID YOU KNOW
Cherries are grown extensively in Germany and form the base of many of the most renowned desserts such as the delicious Black Forest cherry gâteau.

●335 calories per portion

Cherry duckling

SERVES 4
4 duckling portions (see Buying guide)
salt

SAUCE
¾ cup Bing cherry conserve
¼ teaspoon ground cinnamon
⅔ cup red wine

FOR GARNISH
1 package (about 3oz) salted plain potato chips
few watercress sprigs (optional)

1 Preheat the oven to 350°.
2 Pat the duckling portions dry with kitchen paper. Prick the skin with a fork and sprinkle with salt (see Cook's tips).
3 Place the duckling, skin side up, on a rack in a shallow roasting pan. Roast in the oven for about 1¼ hours or until tender and cooked through (the juices should run clear when the thickest part of flesh is pierced with a skewer).
4 During the last 15 minutes cooking, spread the potato chips for the garnish on a baking sheet. Heat through in oven with duckling.
5 Meanwhile, make the sauce: Place the cherry conserve in a heavy saucepan. Stir in the cinnamon and red wine, then bring to a boil, stirring. Lower the heat and simmer gently for about 10 minutes, stirring frequently.
6 Arrange the duckling on a warmed serving dish and garnish with the hot potato chips and watercress, if liked. Serve at once, with the cherry sauce poured over or passed separately.

Cook's Notes

TIME
Preparation is only 5 minutes, cooking time about 1¼ hours, including making the sauce.

COOK'S TIPS
Pricking the duckling skin allows the fat to run during cooking so basting is unnecessary. Sprinkling with salt gives crisp brown skin.

SERVING IDEAS
Serve with puréed potatoes and sliced zucchini sprinkled with a little chopped fresh mint.

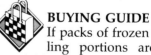
BUYING GUIDE
If packs of frozen duckling portions are unavailable, use 4 chicken portions instead — reduce the cooking time to 1 hour and omit the potato chip garnish.

●700 calories per portion

Cherry layer

SERVES 4

½ lb Bing cherries, pitted
2 tablespoons butter or margarine, at room temperature
6 large slices white or wholewheat bread, crusts removed, if wished (see Economy)
3 tablespoons sugar
2 eggs
1¼ cups milk
2-3 drops vanilla
extra butter or margarine, for greasing

1 Generously grease a 4 cup shallow pie plate.
2 Butter the bread, then cut each slice diagonally in half. Arrange 6 bread triangles, buttered side up and overlapping if necessary, over the base of the prepared dish. Scatter the prepared cherries over the buttered bread, then sprinkle over 2 tablespoons sugar.
3 Add remaining bread triangles and sprinkle over the rest of the sugar. Do not worry if a few cherries show around the edge of the dish or between the bread slices.
4 Beat the eggs with the milk and vanilla and strain over the bread. Leave the pudding to stand in a cool place for 30 minutes.
5 Meanwhile, preheat the oven to 350°.
6 Bake the pudding in the oven for 40-45 minutes, until set and lightly browned. Serve the cherry layer pudding at once, while it is still puffed up.

Cook's Notes

TIME
20 minutes preparation (including pitting the cherries), plus 30 minutes standing and about 45 minutes baking time.

ECONOMY
This is an excellent way of using up dry bread.

● 280 calories per portion

VARIATIONS
When fresh cherries are not in season, use a well drained can (about 16 oz) of pitted cherries instead.
Add ½ teaspoon ground cinnamon to egg and milk mixture.

SERVING IDEAS
Sprinkle the pudding with sugar and serve with cream or vanilla sauce.

Coconut and carrot salad

SERVES 4-6
⅔ cup shredded coconut
1 lb carrots
juice of 1 orange
juice of 1 lemon

1 Grate the carrots using either a 4-sided grater or food processor (see Cook's tip). Put the grated carrots in a large bowl.
2 Mix the orange and lemon juice together, then pour over the carrots. Toss the salad well.
3 Transfer the carrots and juice to a salad bowl or divide the salad between individual serving dishes and sprinkle over the coconut.

4 Chill the carrot and coconut salad in the refrigerator for at least 1 hour or until ready to serve.

Cook's Notes

 TIME
The salad takes 10 minutes to prepare, plus chilling time.

SERVING IDEAS
Serve this refreshingly tangy salad with cold roast chicken or pork. It is particularly good for slimmers, since no sweetening is necessary. Coconut shells make unusual serving dishes.

 COOK'S TIP
To make grating easier, crisp the carrots by soaking them whole in ice water for 1 hour before.

VARIATION
Toss the salad in an oil and vinegar dressing instead of the lemon and orange juice mixture.

●120 calories per portion

Coconut soufflé

SERVES 6-8

2 cans (4 oz each) sweetened moist
   shredded coconut
1 cup warm water
6 eggs, separated
⅓ cup sugar
2 envelopes unflavored gelatin
¼ cup cold water
2 limes (see Preparation)
¼ cup shredded coconut

1 Soak the sweetened coconut in
the warm water for 2 hours, then
put through a blender to make a
cream. Turn into a pan and heat
until almost boiling. Remove from
heat.
2 Put the egg yolks and sugar in a
heatproof bowl that will fit over a
pan of water. Beat together until
thick and pale, then stir in the
warmed coconut cream until
thoroughly mixed in.
3 Set the bowl over a pan of barely
simmering water and cook, stirring
constantly, for about 10 minutes
until the mixture is smooth and
slightly thickened. Remove the
bowl from the heat.
4 Sprinkle the gelatin over the
water in a heatproof bowl. Leave to
soak for 5 minutes until spongy,
then stand the bowl in the pan of
gently simmering water for 1-2
minutes, stirring occasionally, until
the gelatin has dissolved.
5 Beat the gelatin into the coconut
cream mixture, together with the
lime rind. Let mixture cool for about
30 minutes.
6 Meanwhile, tie a paper collar
around a 4 cup soufflé mold, so that
it stands above the rim.
7 In a spotlessly clean, dry bowl,
beat the egg whites until they stand
in stiff peaks, then fold into the
cooled coconut cream mixture.
Transfer to the prepared soufflé
mold and refrigerate for at least 3
hours until set.
8 Meanwhile, brown the remaining
shredded coconut: Put the coconut
on a foil-covered broiler pan and
toast under a fairly hot broiler for 2
minutes, turning constantly, until
evenly browned.
9 Carefully remove the paper collar
from the soufflé, then, using a
spatula, gently press the toasted
coconut onto the exposed side of
the soufflé. Decorate the top
of the soufflé with lime slices and
serve at once.

Cook's Notes

TIME
Preparation takes 1
hour, plus 30 minutes
cooling and at least 3 hours
chilling.

PREPARATION
Finely grate the rind
from 1½ limes, then cut
the remaining half into very
thin slices for decorating — cut
into the center of each slice to
make twists.

SERVING IDEAS
Serve the soufflé with
small cookies for a crisp
contrast.

●680 calories per portion

Cranberry and apple layer

SERVES 4-6

1½ cups all-purpose flour
1 teaspoon baking powder
⅓ cup shredded beef suet
¼ cup sugar
6-7 tablespoons cold water
butter, for greasing

FILLING

2 tablespoons butter
1 cup cranberries, thawed if frozen
1 lb tart apples, pared, quartered, cored and sliced
4-6 tablespoons sugar
finely grated rind of 1 small orange

1 Make the filling: Melt the butter in a heavy-bottomed saucepan. Add the cranberries and apples, cover and cook gently for 20-30 minutes, until apples are tender.

2 Meanwhile, grease a 5 cup pudding mold. Cut a circle of waxed paper or foil 3 inches larger all around than top of mold. Grease 1 side, then make a ½ inch pleat down the center.

3 Remove fruit mixture from heat. Sweeten to taste with sugar, then stir in the orange rind. Set aside.

4 Make the pastry: Sift the flour and baking powder into a bowl. Stir in suet and sugar; add enough water to make a soft dough.

5 Divide the pastry into 4 pieces of graduated size. Roll out smallest piece, place in base of the mold and press gently. Cover with one-third of the fruit mixture. Roll out next largest piece of pastry, place in mold and cover with another third of fruit. Repeat, ending with largest piece of pastry. ⚠

6 Place covering, greased side down, on top of mold and tie securely in place. Place in a heavy kettle or Dutch oven, add boiling water to come halfway up side of mold. Cover, boil gently for 2 hours, topping up water level with more boiling water as necessary.

7 Protecting your hands with pot holders, lift mold out and remove covering. Loosen the pudding with a spatula, then turn out onto a warmed serving plate and serve.

Cook's Notes

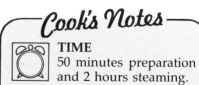

⏰ **TIME**
50 minutes preparation and 2 hours steaming.

⚠ **WATCHPOINT**
Make sure that the last layer of pastry completely covers the fruit mixture and is pressed firmly against the sides of the mold.

●435 calories per portion

Cranberry pork

SERVES 4
3½ lb boneless pork shoulder butt

STUFFING
2 teaspoons vegetable oil
½ onion, finely chopped
2 bacon slices, chopped
1 cup finely chopped mushrooms
2 cups soft white bread crumbs
1 tablespoon finely chopped fresh
    parsley
salt
freshly ground black pepper
a little beaten egg

CRANBERRY SAUCE
thinly pared rind and juice of 1
    small orange
juice of 1 small lemon
¼ cup cranberry sauce
2 teaspoons dry red wine
1 tablespoon cornstarch
2 tablespoons water

1 Preheat the oven to 375°.
2 Make the stuffing: Heat the oil in a skillet, add the onion and bacon and cook over moderate heat for 2 minutes. Add the mushrooms and cook for a further 2-3 minutes, then turn the mixture into a bowl. Stir in the bread crumbs and parsley and season well with salt and pepper. Stir in enough beaten egg just to bind. !
3 Place pork on a working surface and spread the stuffing on it. Roll up tightly and tie securely in several places with fine twine. Calculate the cooking time at 35 minutes per 1 lb plus 35 minutes. Place in a roasting pan, fat side up.
4 Rub the fat all over with salt and pepper. Roast in the oven for the calculated time.
5 About 10 minutes before the end of cooking time, make the cranberry sauce: Cut the pared orange rind into thin strips and simmer for 5 minutes in water. Drain, rinse under cold running water and reserve. Pour the orange and lemon juices into a small pan, add the cranberry sauce and red wine and heat, stirring, until the cranberry sauce has melted.
6 Blend the cornstarch with the water in a cup and stir into the cranberry mixture in the pan. Bring to a boil, stirring. Lower the heat and simmer for about 2 minutes. Spoon the cranberry sauce into a serving bowl, then sprinkle over the reserved orange rind.

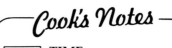
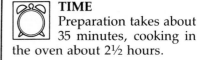
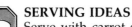

Cook's Notes

TIME
Preparation takes about 35 minutes, cooking in the oven about 2½ hours.

SERVING IDEAS
Serve with carrot sticks tossed in chopped parsley, and pan-roasted potatoes.

COOK'S TIP
To save time, the mushroom stuffing and cranberry sauce can be prepared the previous day, cooled and stored, covered, in the refrigerator.

WATCHPOINT
Add just enough egg to bind the stuffing ingredients: The mixture should not be sloppy.

●655 calories per portion

7 Place the cooked roast on a warmed serving dish and remove the twine.
8 To serve: Carve the roast into neat slices and serve with the cranberry sauce passed separately.

Date crunch layer

SERVES 6-8
1¼ cups chopped dates
¼ cup water
3-4 teaspoons ground cinnamon
¾ cup butter
¼ cup soft brown sugar
1¼ cups rolled oats
1 cup wholewheat flour
margarine, for greasing

1 Preheat the oven to 350° and thoroughly grease an 8 inch layer cake pan.
2 Put the chopped dates in a sauce-pan with the water and cinnamon. Cook gently for about 5 minutes, or until the dates are soft and will spread. Remove the pan from the heat. ⚠
3 Put the butter and sugar into a clean pan and heat gently until the butter has melted. Remove from the heat, sprinkle in the oats and flour and stir to mix in thoroughly.
4 Spread half the oat mixture over the base of the prepared pan then cover with the dates, spreading them evenly. Spread the remaining oat mixture over the top. Bake in the oven for 30 minutes.
5 Remove from the oven and let cool for 10 minutes, then mark into wedges. Leave until completely cold in the pan (see Cook's tip).

Cook's Notes

TIME
Preparation 10 minutes, cooking 30 minutes.

WATCHPOINT
If the date mixture is too dry, add another tablespoon of water.

COOK'S TIP
If you do not want to serve the layer im-mediately, cover the pan with foil — in this way it will keep fresh for up to 2 days.

●460 calories per portion

Fig and pineapple fritters

SERVES 4-6

1 can (about 16 oz) figs in syrup
1 can (about 8 oz) pineapple rings
   in natural juice
all-purpose flour, for dusting
sugar, for sifting

BATTER

¾ cup all-purpose flour
1 teaspoon sugar
1 small egg, beaten
½ teaspoon vegetable oil
6 tablespoons water
vegetable oil, for deep-frying

SAUCE

1 tablespoon cornstarch
2 tablespoons soft brown sugar
2 tablespoons rum or brandy

1 Drain the syrup from the figs and
the juice from the pineapple into a
measuring cup and make up to 1¼
cups, if necessary, with cold water.
Reserve for the sauce.
2 Pat the figs and pineapple rings
dry on kitchen paper, then set them
aside on a fresh piece of kitchen
paper.
3 Make the batter: Sift the flour into
a bowl, stir in the sugar, then add
the egg and the ½ teaspoon oil.
Gradually beat in the water.
4 Make the sauce: Mix the cornstarch and sugar and blend to a
smooth paste with a little of the
measured fruit juice. Heat the remaining juice in a small saucepan,
then gradually stir into the paste.
Return the mixture to the pan and
bring slowly to a boil, stirring constantly. Simmer for 2-3 minutes,
stirring until thick and smooth.
Cover and keep hot.
5 Pour enough vegetable oil into a
deep-fat fryer to come one-third of
the way up the side of the pan. Heat
the oil to 375°. (If you do not have a
cooking thermometer, drop 1 teaspoon batter into the oil — it should
immediately rise to the surface and
start to bubble.)
6 Sprinkle the fruits lightly on both
sides with flour to dry them. Dip
the pineapple rings, one by one,
into the batter and allow any excess
batter to run back into the bowl. Fry

the rings in batches  in the hot oil
for 6-8 minutes, turning them once,
until crisp and golden. Drain on
kitchen paper and keep hot. Coat,
fry and drain the figs in batches in
the same way until golden.
7 Pile the fritters up in a warmed
serving dish. Sift with sugar and
serve at once, with the hot sauce
passed separately.

Cook's Notes

TIME
Preparation and cook-
ing take 40-50 minutes.

WATCHPOINT
Fry the fruits in batches
so that you do not over
crowd the pan. Check the
temperature of the oil before
you add a new batch of fritters
and reheat it, if necessary, to a
temperature of 375°.

ECONOMY
Try using dried figs:
They are a much more
economical alternative to
canned ones. Cover them in
cold tea and soak 1 hour, then
simmer for 30 minutes until
tender. Drain them well, reserving cooking juices to use instead
of the syrup, for the sauce.

●375 calories per portion

21

Gooseberry pie

SERVES 4
½ lb basic pie dough, thawed if
   frozen
little beaten egg, for glazing
sugar, for dredging
heavy cream, to serve

FILLING
½ lb gooseberries, trimmed if
   fresh, thawed and well drained
   if frozen
2 tablespoons fresh white bread
   crumbs (see Cook's tips)
2 tablespoons sugar
½ teaspoon finely chopped fresh
   mint (optional)

1 Preheat the oven to 400°.
2 Cut off one-third of the dough
and reserve. On a lightly floured
surface, roll out remaining dough
and use to line a 9 inch pie plate.
3 Mix the gooseberries with the
bread crumbs, sugar and mint, if
using. Spoon into the dough-lined
plate and spread evenly. Brush the
edges of the dough with water.

4 Use the reserved dough to make a
lattice decoration over the pie (see
Preparation). Brush the dough lattice with beaten egg.
5 Bake the pie in the oven, just
above the center, for 20 minutes;
then lower the heat to 375° and bake
for about 15 minutes more, until the

gooseberries are tender (see Cook's
tips). Cover the top with waxed
paper if the dough is browning too
quickly.
6 Remove the tart from the oven
and sift sugar thickly over the top.
Serve hot, warm or cold, with
heavy cream.

Cook's Notes

TIME
30 minutes preparation,
plus about 35 minutes
baking.

COOK'S TIPS
Bread crumbs absorb
the juices produced by
the filling during baking and
help prevent the dough becom-
ing soggy.
   Use a fine skewer to test that
the gooseberries are tender.

VARIATIONS
Fresh mint gives a
pleasant flavor to
gooseberries, but you could use
a little grated orange or lemon
rind, or ¼ teaspoon apple pie
spice instead.

PREPARATION
A lattice is a very de-
corative way of topping
a pie. If using a very soft or
moist filling, make the lattice on
waxed paper, then gently shake
it onto the pie.
   For a scalloped effect, the
strips can be cut with a pastry
wheel. A plain lattice is made as
follows: Roll out the dough to a
rectangle, ½ inch larger than
diameter of the pie plate. Cut in
½ inch wide strips. Place half
the strips over the tart in
parallel lines. Lay the remaining strips in parallel lines across
the first set. Trim the edges
and press to seal.

•345 calories per portion

Gooseberry puff

SERVES 4
**1 lb gooseberries, trimmed if fresh,
  thawed if frozen (see Cook's tip)**
½ cup sugar

TOPPING
2 eggs, separated
⅔ cup dairy sour cream
½ cup ground almonds
2 tablespoons sugar
**2 tablespoons all-purpose flour,
  sifted**

1 Preheat the oven to 350°.
2 Place the gooseberries in a 5 cup soufflé mold or other ovenproof dish. Sprinkle in the sugar and mix well. Cover the mold and bake in the oven for about 30 minutes, or until the gooseberries are slightly softened and a thin syrup has formed (see Cook's tips).
3 About 5 minutes before the end of cooking time, make the topping: Beat the egg yolks together with a wooden spoon. Slowly beat in the cream, almonds, sugar and flour.
4 In a clean dry bowl, beat the egg whites until standing in stiff peaks. Using a large metal spoon, fold the egg whites into the egg yolk and almond mixture.
5 Spoon the topping evenly over the gooseberries. Return to the oven and bake for a further 30 minutes, or until the topping is risen and golden. Serve at once, while topping is light and puffy.

Grape layer cake

MAKES 6-8 SLICES
¾ cup all-purpose flour
pinch of salt
pinch of baking powder
3 large eggs
½ cup sugar
vegetable oil, for greasing

FILLING AND DECORATION
1¼ cups heavy or whipping cream
3 tablespoons kirsch
2 teaspoons confectioners' sugar, sifted
½ lb seedless grapes, halved, or purple grapes, halved and seeded
½ cup crushed macaroons
ratafias to decorate (optional)

1 Preheat the oven to 375°. Grease a 13 × 9 × 2½ inch oblong baking pan. Line pan with waxed paper and grease the paper.
2 Sift the flour with the salt and baking powder and set aside.
3 Put the eggs and sugar into a large heatproof bowl. Set the bowl over a pan half full of gently simmering water. [!] Using a rotary or hand-held electric beater, beat the mixture until thick and foamy. Continue beating until the mixture is thick enough to hold the trail of the beaters for about 3 seconds when beaters are lifted.
4 Remove the bowl from the pan and beat for a few minutes more until the mixture is cool. Using a large metal spoon, fold in the sifted flour, one-third at a time.
5 Pour mixture into the prepared baking pan and spread evenly by gently tilting the pan. Bake the cake immediately in the oven 15-20 minutes until the surface is golden and springy to the touch. Leave to stand in the pan for 1-2 seconds, then turn out onto a wire rack. Peel off the lining paper and leave to cool completely.
6 Make filling: Whip cream with kirsch and sugar until standing in soft peaks. Spoon half the whipped cream into another bowl and fold in three-quarters of the prepared grapes.
7 Assemble the cake: Cut sponge across into 3 equal rectangles, then sandwich them together with the grape and cream mixture in between. Spread three-quarters of the remaining whipped cream over the top and side. Transfer to a serving plate.
8 Using a spatula, press the crushed macaroons over the side of the layer cake. Put the remaining cream into a pastry bag fitted with a large star tip and pipe a border around the top edge. Decorate with the remaining grapes and the macaroons, if liked. Keep in a cool place and serve within 2 hours.

Cook's Notes

TIME
35-40 minutes, plus cooling and assembling.

WATCHPOINT
If using an electric table mixer there is no need to place bowl over hot water. If beating over hot water, check that the bottom of the bowl does not touch the water or the eggs will scramble.

• 480 calories per slice

Grape syllabub

SERVES 6-8
1 lb grapes, halved with seeds removed
1 cup coarsely crushed macaroons (see Economy)
2 large egg whites
½ cup sugar
½ cup medium dry white wine (see Economy)
2 tablespoons brandy or sherry
1¼ cups heavy cream
2 Chinese gooseberries, peeled and sliced, to decorate

1 Divide half the grapes equally between 6-8 tall stemmed dessert glasses, then cover with half the crushed macaroons. Place the rest of the grapes on top and finish with a layer of the remaining macaroons.
2 In a clean, dry, large bowl, beat the egg whites until standing in stiff peaks. Add half the sugar and beat until the meringue is stiff and glossy. Using a large metal spoon, fold in the remaining sugar. Gradually fold and stir in the wine and brandy.
3 In a separate large bowl, whip the cream until just thickened. Stir the frothy meringue mixture, then beat into the cream, about one-third at a time. Pour the syllabub over the macaroons and grapes, cover the glasses with plastic wrap and refrigerate for 1-2 hours, until the macaroons are moistened and well softened.
4 Just before serving, top each syllabub with slices of Chinese gooseberries. (If added too far in advance, the slices will lose their freshness.) Serve chilled.

Cook's Notes

TIME
55 minutes preparation (including 25 minutes seeding the grapes), plus chilling time.

ECONOMY
Any brittle almond or hazelnut cookies can be used instead of macaroons.

If you do not want to open a large bottle of wine specially for this dessert, buy a miniature bottle.

? DID YOU KNOW
A syllabub is a traditional English dessert, originally made from very fresh milk or cream, and alcohol.

! WATCHPOINT
The dessert needs to be chilled, but do not leave it too long or liquid will collect in base of the glass. This will certainly spoil the appearance, although not the flavor, of the dish.

●470 calories per portion

Grapefruit ice

SERVES 4
grated rind and juice of 2 grapefruit
1 cup caster sugar
1¼ cups water
2 grapefruit slices, quartered, to decorate

1 Place the sugar and water in a saucepan and heat gently until the sugar has dissolved, then bring to a boil and boil for about 5 minutes, without stirring, until a thick syrup is formed.
2 Remove the syrup from the heat and leave until completely cold. 🔲
3 Add the grapefruit rind and juice to the cold syrup and pour into a 5 cup shallow freezerproof container or loaf pan. Freeze in the freezer compartment of a refrigerator or in the freezer for about 30 minutes (see Cook's tip) until the grapefruit mixture is slushy.
4 Remove from the freezer and stir well with a metal spoon until evenly blended.
5 Return to the freezer for 30 minutes, then stir again. Repeat this process once more, then cover and freeze for at least 8 hours. ✳
6 To serve: Stir the mixture well, to break up any large pieces of ice, then spoon into glasses or small dishes. Decorate each portion with quartered grapefruit slices. Serve at once.

Cook's Notes

TIME
15 minutes preparation plus cooling time. Total freezing time is 9½ hours.

WATCHPOINT
The syrup must be completely cold before placing in the freezer.

SERVING IDEAS
This refreshing ice is ideal served after a rich meal, with cookies.

COOK'S TIP
If using the freezer compartment of the refrigerator, turn it to its coldest setting 1 hour in advance.

FREEZING
To save time, prepare the ice well in advance. Seal, label and freeze for up to 3 months. To serve: Proceed as for stage 6.

●130 calories per portion

Lemon chicken

SERVES 4
3-3½ lb broiler/fryer, with giblets
salt
1 onion
1 thin strip lemon rind
1 celery stalk, sliced
4 large carrots, quartered
bouquet garni
2½ cups water

SAUCE
2 tablespoons butter or margarine
4 tablespoons all-purpose flour
juice of 1 lemon
1 egg
2 tablespoons light cream
pinch of turmeric
freshly ground black pepper
lemon slices, parsley sprigs and olives, for garnish (optional)

1 Pat the chicken dry with kitchen paper and sprinkle it inside and out with salt. Insert the onion into the body cavity, then truss with thread or fine twine.

2 Place the chicken and giblets (see Cook's tip) in a large flameproof casserole with remaining ingredients around it. Pour in the water and sprinkle in 1 teaspoon salt. Place over moderate heat.

3 Bring to a boil, skim off any foam that rises to the surface, then lower the heat, cover and simmer for 1¼ hours or until chicken is tender (the juices should run clear when the thickest part of the thigh is pierced with a skewer).

4 Using a slotted spoon and a carving fork, remove the chicken, draining it over the pan, then place on a warmed serving dish. Remove the trussing thread and onion.

5 Strain the cooking liquid, discarding the giblets but reserving the vegetables, and measure 2 cups. Place the vegetables around the chicken and keep hot.

6 To make the sauce: Melt the butter in a small saucepan, sprinkle in the flour and stir over low heat for 1-2 minutes until straw-colored. Gradually stir in the measured broth, then bring to a boil, lower the heat and simmer gently for 2 minutes, stirring. Off heat, let cool slightly.

7 In a bowl, beat the lemon juice and egg together until the mixture is frothy, then beat into the sauce a little at a time.

8 Place the pan over gentle heat, stir in the cream and turmeric [!] and heat through. Taste and adjust seasoning, then pour a little over the chicken. Garnish with lemon slices, parsley sprigs and olives, if liked. Serve at once, with the remaining sauce.

Cook's Notes

TIME
Preparation takes 15 minutes and cooking 1 hour. Last-minute preparation of sauce will take 5-10 minutes.

COOK'S TIP
Remove the liver from the chicken giblets or the broth will taste bitter.

[!] WATCHPOINT
Take care not to boil the sauce or it may curdle.

[?] DID YOU KNOW
Turmeric is a tropical herb of the ginger family. It is usually sold as an aromatic yellow powder.

●475 calories per portion

Lemon chiffon

SERVES 4-6
grated rind and juice of 1 lemon
1 envelope unflavored gelatin
¼ cup warm water
3 eggs, separated
½ cup sugar
2 tablespoons dairy sour cream or
  half and half

1 In a small pan, sprinkle the gelatin onto the warm water and leave until spongy (see Cook's tips).
2 Put the egg yolks and sugar into a small bowl. Stand the bowl in hot water and beat until very light and fluffy, until the mixture dropping from the beater leaves a trail behind it when lifted.

3 Stir in the lemon rind and juice and sour cream.
4 Melt the spongy gelatin mixture over low heat and stir it into the yolk mixture (see Cook's tips).
5 Cool the lemon mixture until it is just on the point of setting.
6 Stiffly beat the egg whites and fold them into the mixture.
7 Pour the mixture into a serving bowl and put it into a cool place or the refrigerator to set.

Cook's Notes

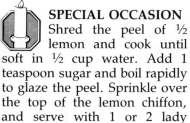

TIME
Preparation 45 minutes, and allow at least 1 hour for the lemon chiffon to set.

COOK'S TIPS
If an electric beater is used there is no need to stand the bowl in hot water. To get the eggs to the proper texture will take about 5 minutes.

Always add gelatin powder to the liquid, not the other way around. Melt over the lowest heat, and when you add the melted gelatin stir all the time.

SPECIAL OCCASION
Shred the peel of ½ lemon and cook until soft in ½ cup water. Add 1 teaspoon sugar and boil rapidly to glaze the peel. Sprinkle over the top of the lemon chiffon, and serve with 1 or 2 lady fingers per serving.

● 185 calories per portion

Lemon fish salad

SERVES 4
4 thin cod or haddock fillets (total weight 2 lb), skinned
2 tablespoons all-purpose flour
salt and freshly ground black pepper
¼ cup butter or margarine

DRESSING
1 onion, finely chopped
2 tomatoes, finely chopped
1 cup fresh bread crumbs
grated rind and juice of 1 lemon
¾ cup salad oil

FOR GARNISH
chopped chives
fennel and lemon slices and grated lemon rind (optional)

1 Place the flour in a plastic bag and season with salt and pepper.

2 Wash the fish and pat dry with kitchen paper. Place the fish in the bag and shake gently to coat.
3 Melt the butter in a large skillet, add the fish fillets in a single layer and cook over moderate heat for 5 minutes on each side until cooked through and lightly browned (see Cook's tip). Remove the fish from the pan with a slotted spatula and place on a serving platter. Set aside to cool.
4 Meanwhile, make the dressing: Put all the ingredients in a bowl and stir until well combined. Add salt and pepper to taste.
5 Spoon dressing over the fish; garnish with chives, fennel and lemon slices and rind, if liked. Serve chilled or at room temperature.

Cook's Notes

TIME
This dish takes 30 minutes to prepare and cook. Allow a little extra time for the fish to cool.

FOR CHILDREN
The flavor of the dressing may be too sharp and pronounced for children, but they will love the cold fish served with mayonnaise or even catsup.

SERVING IDEAS
Serve with cold, sliced or whole, new potatoes, and a fennel salad.

COOK'S TIP
So that the fish looks at its best when cooked, cook the top sides of the fillets first, then turn them over and cook the skinned sides.

●715 calories per portion

Lemon and lentil soup

SERVES 4
grated rind and juice of 1 lemon
½ cup split red lentils
1 tablespoon butter or margarine
2 celery stalks, chopped
1 medium onion, finely chopped
1 quart boiling water
4 chicken bouillon cubes
¼ teaspoon ground cumin
(optional)
salt and freshly ground black pepper
1 red pepper, seeded and thinly
sliced into rings

FOR GARNISH
1 lemon, thinly sliced
chopped chives (optional)

1 Melt the butter in a saucepan, add the celery and onion, then cover and cook gently for 4 minutes.
2 Remove the pan from the heat, then stir in the lentils and water, with bouillon cubes. Add the lemon rind and juice, and the cumin, if using. Season to taste with salt and pepper. Cover and simmer over gentle heat for 30 minutes.
3 Add the sliced pepper to the pan, cover and cook for a further 30 minutes. Taste and adjust seasoning.
4 Pour the soup into warmed serving bowls, float the lemon slices on top, then sprinkle over the chives if using. Serve at once.

Cook's Notes

TIME
Preparation takes about 20 minutes; cooking takes 1 hour.

FREEZING
Cool quickly, then freeze without the lemon and chives in a rigid plastic container or freezer bag (do not use foil containers, or the acid in the soup may react against the foil). Seal, label and freeze for up to 6 months. Thaw at room temperature, then reheat until bubbling, adding a little more water if necessary.

SERVING IDEAS
Warm crusty rolls are ideal to serve with this soup. For a luxurious touch, top each serving with 1 tablespoon dairy sour cream.

VARIATIONS
For a lentil and orange soup, use 2 small oranges instead of lemons.
If chives are unavailable, use chopped scallion tops or parsley, if using another garnish as well as the lemon.

●135 calories per portion

Lemon potatoes

SERVES 6
grated rind and juice of 1 lemon
2 lb potatoes, cut into 1 inch
  cubes
3 tablespoons butter
1 onion, finely chopped
salt and freshly ground black pepper

1 Preheat the oven to 375°.
2 Put the potatoes into a large saucepan, cover with cold water and bring to a boil. Reduce heat and simmer for 3 minutes. ⚠ Drain well.
3 Melt the butter in the rinsed-out pan, add the onion and cook gently until soft but not colored. Stir in the lemon rind and juice and season to taste with salt and pepper.

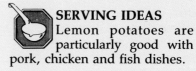

Cook's Notes

⏰ **TIME**
Preparation takes about 20 minutes, cooking in the oven about 1 hour.

❗ **WATCHPOINT**
Do not simmer the potatoes for longer than 3 minutes, or they will break up when tossed in the lemon-flavored butter, and the finished dish will be mushy.

●185 calories per portion

👨‍🍳 **COOK'S TIP**
This is a perfect way of cooking potatoes for a supper party, as the potatoes can be prepared up to the end of stage 4, turned into a shallow ovenproof dish and refrigerated overnight. About 1 hour before serving, bake them in the oven.

🥄 **SERVING IDEAS**
Lemon potatoes are particularly good with pork, chicken and fish dishes.

4 Return the drained potatoes to the pan and carefully turn them with a spatula until they are thoroughly coated with the lemon-flavored butter.
5 Turn the potatoes into a large shallow ovenproof dish, arranging them in a single layer (see Cook's tip). Bake in the oven for 50-60 minutes until golden and crisp on top. Serve the potatoes hot, straight from the dish.

Lime icebox loaf

SERVES 10
grated rind of 2 limes
juice of 3 limes
3 eggs, separated
½ cup sugar
2 cups heavy cream
8 vanilla wafers, crushed
fresh lime slices, to decorate

1 Line the base of a 5 cup loaf pan with waxed paper.
2 Put the eggs yolks in a large heatproof bowl over a pan half full of gently simmering water. Using a rotary or hand-held electric mixer, slowly beat in the sugar until pale and thick. ⚠️ Remove from heat and stir in lime rind and juice.
3 Whip the cream until standing in soft peaks and fold into the lime mixture.
4 In a clean, dry bowl and using clean beaters, beat the egg whites until standing in soft peaks. Using a large metal spoon, fold the egg whites into the lime mixture.
5 Sprinkle a thin layer of wafer crumbs over the bottom of the pan. Carefully pour in the lime mixture and top with a layer of the remaining crumbs.
6 Cover with foil, then place in the freezer compartment of the refrigerator or in the freezer and freeze for about 8 hours, or overnight, until firm. ❄️
7 To serve (see Cook's tip): Uncover the pan, then run a slim spatula around the edges of the loaf to loosen it. Turn out onto a flat serving plate and carefully remove the waxed paper. Decorate the loaf with slices of lime and serve at once.

Cook's Notes

⏰ TIME
Preparation takes 40 minutes, plus about 8 hours freezing time.

👨‍🍳 COOK'S TIP
If you do not want to serve all the pudding at once, cut off as many slices as you need, then wrap the (undecorated) surplus in foil and return it to the freezer for up to 1 month.

❗ WATCHPOINT
Make sure that the egg yolks and sugar are really thick before removing from the heat.

❄️ FREEZING
Freeze at the end of stage 6. Overwrap and return to the freezer for up to 1 month.

●365 calories per portion

Lime marmalade

MAKES ABOUT 5 LB
1½ lb limes (see Cook's tips), stalk
 ends trimmed
6 cups water
juice of ½ lemon
6 cups sugar

1 Put the limes into a large, heavy-bottomed saucepan. Pour in the water and bring to a boil, then cover and simmer over gentle heat for about 1½ hours, until the fruit is completely soft when pierced with a knife.
2 Remove from the heat. Using a slotted spoon, transfer the limes, one at a time, to a plate. (Reserve the cooking water.) Hold each fruit steady with a fork and cut into quarters with a sharp knife, then finely shred or chop the peel.
3 Put all the chopped peel and juices from the plate into a preserving pan. Add the water in which the limes were cooked, the lemon juice

and sugar. Clip a candy thermometer, if using, to the pan.
4 Stir over low heat until the sugar has dissolved, then bring to a boil. Cook at a rolling boil, stirring occasionally, for 15 minutes (see Cook's tips) or until thermometer registers 221°.

5 Remove from the heat, let cool for 15 minutes, then ladle into hot, sterilized jars (see Cook's tips). Seal and leave the marmalade to cool completely.
6 Store the jars of marmalade in a cool, dry place and use within 9 months of making.

Mango boats

SERVES 6

½ lb basic pie dough, thawed if frozen
2 large fresh mangoes (see Buying guide)
2 tablespoons apricot or peach jam
1 tablespoon water

PASTRY CREAM
2 egg yolks
¼ cup sugar
1 tablespoon all-purpose flour
1 tablespoon cornstarch
1¼ cups milk
1 tablespoon cherry brandy

1 Roll out the dough on a lightly floured surface and use to line 12 boat-shaped molds, measuring about 4½ × 2 inches at the widest points across the top (see Preparation).

2 Prick the base of each dough case in several places with a fork, then stand the molds on a baking sheet and refrigerate for 20 minutes.

3 Meanwhile, preheat the oven to 400°.

4 Bake the cases in the oven for 15-20 minutes, or until the dough is crisp and golden.

5 Cool the cases in their molds for 5 minutes then ease the cases out of the molds and leave on a wire rack to cool completely.

6 Make the pastry cream: Put the egg yolks in a bowl with the sugar and flours. Stir in a little of the milk to make a creamy consistency.

7 Bring the remaining milk to just below the boiling point, remove from heat and gradually stir into the egg mixture. Pour back into the pan and beat continuously over low heat until the mixture thickens and comes to a boil. Remove from the heat and cover with a piece of dampened waxed paper to prevent a skin forming. Leave until cold.

8 To assemble the boats: Mix the cherry brandy into the cold pastry cream, ⚠ beating well to keep it smooth. Divide the cream between the dough cases, spreading it over them evenly and smoothly.

9 Peel the mangoes, then cut the flesh into ¼ inch thick slices. Place the slices neatly on top of the pastry cream.

10 Strain the apricot jam into a small pan, add the water and stir well over low heat until the jam has melted. Brush the jam over the fruit and leave to set in the refrigerator for at least 2 hours before serving.

Cook's Notes

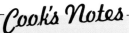

🕐 **TIME**
The mango boats take 1 hour to prepare, plus cooling and chilling time.

🛍 **BUYING GUIDE**
If fresh managoes are unobtainable, use 1 can (about 15 oz) sliced mangoes. Drain and cut as in stage 9.

🔪 **PREPARATION**
To line the molds: Invert mold onto the dough and cut round it, leaving a ¾ inch wide border. Cut out as many as possible, then roll the trimmings and cut out the rest. Lift each lining and lay it loosely over each mold. Press gently in place and trim.

⚠ **WATCHPOINT**
The pastry cream must be cold or the flavor of the liqueur will alter.

🥄 **SERVING IDEAS**
Serve with thickly whipped cream.

● 455 calories per portion

Mango lamb

SERVES 4
2 breasts of lamb, each weighing about 1½ lb, trimmed of excess fat, boned, cut into bite-size pieces (see Buying guide)
1½ tablespoons vegetable oil
1 onion, finely chopped
2 teaspoons ground ginger
1 teaspoon ground coriander
1 tablespoon honey
1 tablespoon Worcestershire sauce
1 tablespoon light soy sauce
¼ cup white wine vinegar
2½ cups beef broth
salt and freshly ground black pepper
4½ teaspoons cornstarch
4½ teaspoons water
1 cup frozen peas
1 large ripe mango, thinly sliced (see Buying guide)
watercress sprigs, for garnish

1 Heat 1 tablespoon of the oil in a large saucepan, add one-third of the lamb pieces and cook over brisk heat, turning, to seal and brown on all sides. Drain on kitchen paper and set aside. Cook remaining lamb pieces in the same way, in 2 batches, to brown and seal.

2 Heat the remaining oil in the pan. Add the onion and cook, stirring, for 2 minutes. Add the ginger and coriander and cook for 30 seconds, stirring once or twice, then remove the pan from heat.

3 Blend together the honey, Worcestershire and soy sauces, vinegar and broth. Pour into the pan, return to heat and bring to a boil. Add the lamb to the pan, season with salt and pepper, then lower heat, cover and simmer for 50 minutes until the lamb is cooked through.

4 Blend the cornstarch with water to make a smooth paste. Stir into the lamb mixture. Bring to a boil, stirring constantly. Add the peas 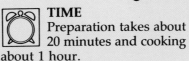 and all but 10 mango slices to the pan and cook gently for a further 10 minutes, stirring once or twice.

5 Spoon onto a warmed serving dish, garnish with the reserved mango slices and the watercress sprigs. Serve at once.

Cook's Notes

TIME
Preparation takes about 20 minutes and cooking about 1 hour.

FREEZING
Do not add the mango. Cool quickly, transfer to a foil container and seal, label and freeze for up to 3 months. To serve: Thaw overnight in the refrigerator, add the mango and heat in a 350° oven until heated through. Finish the dish as in stage 5.

BUYING GUIDE
Lamb breasts are a good economical buy.

Mangoes are available in season from food markets and many supermarkets make a feature of exotic fruit.

However, if fresh mango is unobtainable, use a can (about 15 oz) of mango slices. Drain well before using: Reserve the juice for another use – it makes an unusual syrup for fruit salad.

●1015 calories per portion

35

Mango spoon dessert

SERVES 4-6

2 ripe mangoes, total weight about 1½ lb (see Preparation)

1 can (about 8 oz) pineapple rings in natural juice, drained with ½ cup juice reserved

¼ lb green grapes, halved and seeded

¼ lb purple grapes, halved and seeded

1 Put the mangoes in a blender with their juice and the measured pineapple juice. Blend to a purée, then pour into a large bowl.

2 Cut each pineapple ring into 6 pieces and add to the mango purée together with the grapes. Cover and refrigerate for 30 minutes.

3 Spoon the mixture into 4-6 small dishes. Serve chilled.

Cook's Notes

 TIME
Total preparation time (including chilling) is about 1 hour.

PREPARATION
Prepare each mango as follows:

1 *Using a sharp knife, make 2 cuts across the mango, each about ½ inch from the center, to make 3 sections. The middle section contains the large central seed.*

VARIATION
When fresh mangoes are scarce, use 2 cans (8 oz each) mango slices.

2 *Using a teaspoon, scoop out the flesh from both side sections. Save any juice and add to flesh. Remove skin from central section then cut flesh from seed.*

●135 calories per portion

Mango yogurt foam

SERVES 4

2 large, ripe mangoes, sliced (see Preparation)
1 orange
1 teaspoon unflavored gelatin
3 tablespoons cold water
1¼ cups plain yogurt
2-3 tablespoons confectioners' sugar
1 egg white

1 Using a vegetable parer, pare several strips of rind from the orange. [!] With a small, sharp knife, shred the rind into matchstick-size strips.
2 Bring a small pan of water to a boil and blanch the strips for 2-3 minutes; drain and refresh under cold running water. Drain the strips and pat dry on kitchen paper.

Transfer to a plate and set aside.
3 Squeeze the juice from the orange, then purée the prepared mangoes and orange juice in a blender.
4 Sprinkle the gelatin over the water in a small, heavy-bottomed pan. Leave to soak for 5 minutes, then set over very low heat for 1-2 minutes, until the gelatin is dissolved.
5 Stirring constantly with a wooden spoon, pour the dissolved gelatin in a thin stream onto the mango purée (see Cook's tip). Gradually beat in the yogurt, then sweeten to taste with confectioners' sugar.
6 In a spotlessly clean, dry bowl, beat the egg white until standing in stiff peaks. Using a large metal spoon, fold the egg white into the mango mixture. Taste and fold in more sugar, if necessary.
7 Spoon the foam into 4 dessert dishes or stemmed glasses and decorate with the strips of orange rind. Serve within 2 hours.

Cook's Notes

TIME
Preparation takes about 50 minutes.

WATCHPOINT
Take care to use only the colored rind and not the bitter white pith just beneath it.

PREPARATION
Peel mangoes over a plate (to catch the juices) as shown below, then slice the flesh from the large central seed in large pieces. Scrape any remaining flesh from the skin and add to the slices, together with any juices.

Score the skin lengthwise with a small, sharp knife, dividing it into several sections. Hold a corner of one section between the flat side of the blade and your thumb, then pull the skin away from the flesh. Remove the remaining sections of skin in the same way.

COOK'S TIP
Use a flexible rubber spatula to scrape the last of the dissolved gelatin out of the pan.

VARIATIONS
If fresh mangoes are unavailable, use two cans (about 8 oz each) of well-drained mango slices. Other soft or drained canned fruits can be used instead of mangoes: You will need 1¼ cups of thick purée.

●150 calories per portion

Melon and mandarin salad

sherry to the melon, then pour the lychees, together with their juice, into the bowl. Stir the fruit gently to mix.

3 Cover the bowl with plastic wrap and refrigerate for 2 hours. To serve: Divide the fruit salad between 6 individual bowls.

SERVES 6
1 small honeydew melon
1 can (about 11 oz) mandarins, drained
¼ cup medium-dry sherry
1 can (about 20 oz) lychees

1 Cut the melon in half and scoop out the seeds. Cut the flesh into balls using a melon baller, then put in a glass bowl.
2 Add the drained mandarins and

Cook's Notes

TIME
This delicately-flavored fruit salad only takes 15 minutes preparation, plus chilling time.

VARIATION
Use fresh mandarins and lychees when in season and substitute the canned lychee juice with a sugar syrup: Dissolve ¼ cup sugar in ½ cup water, add the sherry, then boil the syrup mixture for 2-3 minutes. Let syrup cool completely before mixing with the fruit.

The sherry in the salad may be replaced by dry white wine, or, for added zing, by an orange liqueur, such as Cointreau or Triple Sec.

●110 calories per portion

Melon and peach sherbets

SERVES 4-6
1 ripe ogen or cantaloupe melon, weighing about 1½ lb
4 large ripe peaches, peeled and pitted
1 cup sugar
1¼ cups water
3 tablespoons lemon juice
2 egg whites
mint sprigs, for garnish (optional)

1 Put the sugar in a saucepan with the water and stir over low heat until the sugar has dissolved. Bring to a boil, then boil rapidly for 5 minutes, without stirring, until a thick syrup is formed.
2 Remove the syrup from the heat and set aside until completely cold.
3 Halve the melon and remove the seeds. Scoop out the flesh and purée in a blender.

Cook's Notes

TIME
30 minutes preparation, plus cooking the syrup and 2 hours initial freezing. Allow at least 2 hours final freezing, then 30 minutes softening at room temperature.

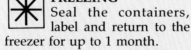 **FREEZING**
Seal the containers, label and return to the freezer for up to 1 month.

BUYING GUIDE
An ogen melon is round in shape with a smooth, speckled skin, divided by stripes of green. To achieve the utmost flavor, the melon must be ripe: It should be strongly scented and feel heavy for its size. The stem end should give slightly.

●305 calories per portion

4 Stir half the cold syrup and half the lemon juice into the melon purée, then transfer the mixture to a rigid container.
5 Purée the peaches in a blender, then stir in the remaining syrup and lemon juice. Transfer the purée to a rigid container.
6 Freeze both mixtures for 2 hours until firm around the edges.
7 In a clean, dry bowl, beat the egg whites until they stand in stiff peaks. Remove the mixtures from the freezer and break up with the beater, then fold half the egg white into the melon mixture and half into the peach mixture. Cover tightly and return to the freezer for at least 2 hours until firm.
8 To serve: Let stand in container at room temperature for about 30 minutes until the sherbet is soft enough to scoop into individual glasses. Garnish with mint, if liked.

Nectarine brulée

SERVES 4-6
3 nectarines (see Buying guide),
peeled, halved, pitted and sliced
grated rind of 1 orange
1 tablespoon orange juice
1¼ cups heavy cream
1 tablespoon confectioners' sugar
⅔ cup plain yogurt
¾ cup light soft brown sugar

1 Arrange the nectarine slices in a 4 cup flameproof glass dish (see Cook's tips). Sprinkle over the orange rind and juice.
2 Whip the cream with the confectioners' sugar until it forms soft peaks. Stir the yogurt until smooth, then fold it into the cream.
3 Spread the cream mixture evenly over the nectarines. Cover and chill in refrigerator for at least 8 hours.
4 Preheat the broiler to high.
5 Uncover the dish and sprinkle the

sugar over the surface, making sure that the cream is completely covered. [!] Level the surface of the sugar with back of a metal spoon.
6 Place the dish under the broiler

close to the heat, for 1-2 minutes, until the sugar is bubbling and caramelized. [!] Let cool, then refrigerate for at least 2 hours. Serve chilled (see Cook's tips).

Cook's Notes

 TIME
25 minutes preparation plus at least 10 hours for cooling and chilling.

 BUYING GUIDE
Nectarines are similar to peaches, but have a firmer texture and smooth skin. When ripe they should feel soft, but not squashy.

If you cannot buy nectarines, use fresh peaches or 1 can (about 15 oz) drained peach slices. Fresh or canned apricots also make a good substitute.

COOK'S TIPS
Use an oven-to-table dish, as the dessert is

taken to the table for serving. Avoid metal which would conduct heat from the broiler to the cream.

To serve, crack the caramel by tapping it with the back of a large metal spoon.

[!] WATCHPOINTS
The sugar must cover the cream completely, right to the edge, or the cream may bubble up under the heat.

Watch the sugar constantly as it can blacken if left a few seconds too long. Turn the dish if necessary so that the sugar caramelizes evenly.

●575 calories per portion

Nectarine tart

MAKES 6 SLICES
½ cup fresh cream cheese (see
   Cook's tip)
1 cup all-purpose flour, sifted
1 tablespoon sugar

FILLING
4 nectarines
1¼ cups water
¼ cup sugar
1 tablespoon lemon juice
¼ cup currant jelly or strained
   apricot jam, for glazing

1 Make the pastry: Beat the cream cheese until soft and smooth. Add the flour and sugar and continue beating until the mixture is evenly crumbly. Using your fingers, draw the mixture together to make a soft dough.
2 Turn the dough out onto a lightly floured surface and knead briefly; wrap in plastic wrap and refrigerate for 1 hour (and up to 24 hours).
3 Preheat the oven to 400°.
4 On a lightly floured surface, roll out the pastry and use to line a loose-bottomed 8 inch fluted flan pan. Prick the base with a fork, then line with a large circle of waxed paper or foil and weight down with pie weights.
5 Bake in the oven for 10 minutes. Remove paper or foil and weights and return to the oven for a further 10-15 minutes until pastry is set and lightly colored. Remove the side of the pan, slide the flan shell onto a wire rack and leave to cool completely.
6 Meanwhile, prepare the filling: Put the water into a heavy-bottomed saucepan with the sugar and lemon juice. Stir over low heat until the sugar has dissolved, then bring to a boil, without stirring, and simmer for 1-2 minutes.
7 Halve and pit the nectarines and lower into the syrup with a slotted spoon. Cover and poach gently for about 5 minutes until just tender. ⚠
Remove the pan from the heat. Lift the nectarines out of the syrup with the slotted spoon and let cool completely. Reserve 1 tablespoon of syrup in the pan.

8 Assemble the tart: Place the flan shell on a serving plate. Skin nectarines, if liked, then cut into thick slices or leave the halves intact and arrange them carefully in the flan shell.

9 Add jelly or jam to reserved syrup and stir well over low heat until melted. Let glaze cool until beginning to thicken, then brush over the nectarines. Leave to set before serving.

Cook's Notes

⏰ TIME
10-15 minutes, plus chilling the pastry, then 1¼ hours, plus setting.

❗ WATCHPOINT
Do not overcook the nectarines: They must keep their shape or the whole look of the tart will be spoiled.

VARIATION
Firm peaches can be used instead. Do not use canned fruit for this recipe.

COOK'S TIP
Pastry made with cream cheese is richer and more crumbly than basic pie dough. There are also fewer calories. It has a delicious flavor which goes beautifully with fresh nectarines, but basic pie dough can be used instead, if you prefer. When using basic pie dough pastry, you will need ⅓ lb dough for an 8 inch fluted flan pan.

●245 calories per slice

Orange bacon slices

SERVES 4
4 thick Canadian bacon slices (see Buying guide)
6 pearl onions, roughly chopped
1 tablespoon soft brown sugar
½ teaspoon ground ginger
freshly ground black pepper
1 large orange
⅔ cup chicken or ham broth
parsley sprigs, for garnish

1 Preheat the oven to 375° (see Economy).
2 In a bowl, mix the onions with the sugar, ginger and pepper to taste (see Cook's tip).
3 Arrange the bacon slices in a shallow ovenproof dish or casserole. Cut orange into 8 sections, saving as much juice as possible, and put 2 on each slice. Sprinkle the sugar mixture evenly over the bacon, then add the broth and any reserved orange juice so that the bacon slices are steeped in the liquid.
4 Cover loosely with foil and bake in the oven on the shelf above center for 35-40 minutes. Garnish with parsley sprigs and serve hot, straight from the dish.

Cook's Notes

 TIME
This dish takes about 50 minutes to prepare and cook.

BUYING GUIDE
If possible, use Canadian bacon slices, each weighing about ¼ lb. These slices are available at most supermarkets.
Alternatively, use smoked pork loin chops instead of the bacon slices.

 ECONOMY
As a time- and cost-saver, the bacon can be cooked in a large skillet, if you have one, on top of the stove. Glaze the bacon under a pre-heated broiler before serving.

COOK'S TIP
Do not add any salt to this dish when cooking as it will be salty enough.

●140 calories per portion

Orange chicken casserole

SERVES 4

3 oranges
4 chicken pieces, each weighing
  about ½ lb
2 tablespoons all-purpose flour (see
  Freezing)
salt and freshly ground black pepper
3 tablespoons vegetable oil
1 onion, finely chopped
⅓ cup chicken broth
1 tablespoon white wine vinegar or
  lemon juice
2 teaspoons dark soft brown sugar
⅔ teaspoon dried sweet basil

1 Put the flour into a plastic bag and season it with salt and pepper. Add the chicken pieces one at a time and shake to coat them thoroughly. Shake off and reserve the excess seasoned flour.
2 With a vegetable parer remove the rind from 1 orange. Strip the pith away and cut the rind into thin matchstick lengths. Set aside. Squeeze the juice from all the oranges and reserve.
3 Preheat the oven to 375°. Heat 1 tablespoon oil in a skillet, add the onion and cook gently for 3 minutes. With a slotted spoon, transfer the cooked onion to a large casserole and set aside.
4 Heat the remaining oil in the skillet, add the chicken pieces and cook over moderate heat for 4-5 minutes on each side until golden brown. Transfer to the casserole with a slotted spoon.
5 Add the reserved seasoned flour to the skillet and stir over low heat for 1-2 minutes. Gradually stir in the orange juice and broth. Raise the heat and bring to a boil, stirring. Add the remaining ingredients and salt and pepper to taste, then pour the sauce over the chicken.
6 Cover the casserole and cook in the oven for 1-1¼ hours or until the chicken is tender (the juices should run clear when the thickest part of the thigh is pierced). ✳
7 Meanwhile, blanch the strips of reserved orange rind by cooking in boiling water for 2 minutes. Drain and reserve for the garnish.
8 Transfer the chicken to a warm serving dish. Taste and adjust seasoning of the sauce, then pour over the chicken pieces. Garnish with the blanched orange strips and serve at once.

Cook's Notes

TIME
40 minutes preparation
1-1¼ hours cooking.
The garnish takes 10 minutes to prepare during cooking time.

✳ FREEZING
Cook the casserole as described, using cornstarch instead of flour for thickening. Cool quickly by setting the casserole in a large bowl of ice water, then flash freeze in the casserole until solid. Remove from the casserole, wrap in foil, then seal, label and return to the freezer. Store for up to 2 months. To serve: Unwrap and return to the casserole, then cover and reheat in a 400° oven for 45 minutes or until heated through and bubbling. Prepare the orange matchstick garnish as described.

●365 calories per portion

Orange and lemon sherbet

SERVES 12
12 oranges (see Buying guide)
8-9 lemons
1 cup water
2 cups sugar
1 egg white

1 Wash the oranges and 3 of the lemons. With a potato peeler, peel the rinds from the 3 lemons thinly, then put them into a saucepan with the water and sugar. Stir over a low heat until the sugar has dissolved, then bring to a boil. Boil for 2 minutes, without stirring, then remove from the heat, cover and let syrup stand for 1 hour.

2 Squeeze all the lemons and measure 1 pint juice, making up the quantity with water. Cut the top third off each orange and squeeze out the juice from the bottom two-thirds. [!] Strain both lemon and orange juices together – you should have about 5 cups.

3 Remove all the remaining flesh from the orange cases (see Preparation). Put the orange cases and "lids" on a tray (see Cook's tip) and put into the freezer.

4 Choose a very large bowl that will fit into the fast-freeze compartment of a freezer.

5 Pour the orange and lemon juice into the bowl then strain in the sugar syrup and stir well.

6 Beat the egg white until soft peaks form, then fold it into the mixture.

7 Freeze the mixture for about 4

hours, until it has frozen to a width of 1 inch around the edge, then remove from the freezer and stir well with a large metal spoon until evenly blended. Return to the freezer and freeze for a further 3 hours or until the sherbet is frozen to a firm mushy consistency, but is not completely hard. Stir with a metal spoon once every hour during this freezing process.

8 Fill the orange cases with the sherbet, mounding it up well on top. Replace the "lids", pressing them in at an angle. Return the oranges to the freezer for 1-2 hours or until the sherbet is frozen.

9 When ready to serve, remove the oranges from the freezer and place on small decorative plates or saucers. Serve at once.

Cook's Notes

TIME
About 2 hours to make and 8-9 hours to freeze.

WATCHPOINT
Be careful not to split the skins of the oranges when squeezing out the juice.

BUYING GUIDE
Choose oranges with good unmarked skins and try to find 12 more or less the same size.

COOK'S TIP
If the orange cases do not stand level, take a very thin slice off the bottoms.

PREPARATION
To remove all flesh from inside the oranges:

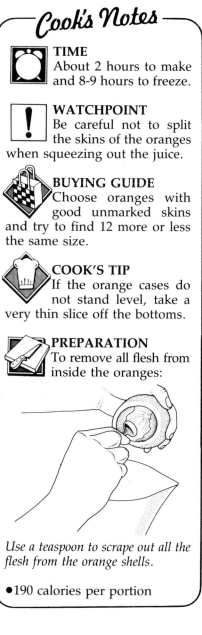

Use a teaspoon to scrape out all the flesh from the orange shells.

● 190 calories per portion

Orange turkey

SERVES 4

**4 turkey fillets or breasts, each
  weighing about ¼ lb, skinned
  (see Buying guide)**
1½ tablespoons all-purpose flour
2 tablespoons sesame seeds
1 teaspoon ground ginger
**grated rind and juice of 2 large
  oranges**
salt and freshly ground black pepper
2 tablespoons butter or margarine
1 tablespoon vegetable oil
1¼ cups chicken broth
½ cup white wine

1 Put the flour, sesame seeds, ground ginger and grated orange rind in a plastic bag and season with salt and pepper.

2 Pat the turkey fillets dry with kitchen paper, then put in the plastic bag and shake until well coated. Reserve any remaining flour.

3 Melt the butter in the oil in a large skillet. Add the turkey and cook over moderate heat for 5 minutes on each side. Remove from the pan with a slotted spoon and keep warm.

4 Add the reserved seasoned flour to the fat in the pan and cook over low heat for 1-2 minutes stirring constantly. Gradually stir in the orange juice, chicken broth and wine, then return the turkey to the pan. Bring to a boil, stirring constantly, then lower the heat and simmer gently for 25-30 minutes until the turkey is cooked through and tender.

5 Transfer the turkey to a warmed serving platter. Taste and adjust seasoning of the sauce, then pour a little sauce over the turkey. Serve the turkey at once with the remaining sauce passed separately in a sauceboat.

Cook's Notes

TIME
Preparation takes about 25 minutes and cooking 25-30 minutes.

SERVING IDEAS
Serve on a bed of boiled rice with a colorful garnish of blanched strips of orange rind, or a few orange slices, peeled and dipped in finely chopped parsley, then cut in half.

VARIATIONS
Chicken breasts or rabbit pieces can be used instead of the turkey, and lemon rind and juice instead of orange.

BUYING GUIDE
Fresh turkey fillets and boneless breasts are available at most large supermarkets. They are an economical cut of meat to buy because they have little or no fat or wastage and cook quickly.

●350 calories per portion

Orange upside-down cake

SERVES 6-8

2 oranges (see Preparation)
½ cup butter or margarine
½ cup sugar
2 eggs, lightly beaten
¼ cup candied cherries, rinsed, dried and chopped
2 tablespoons chopped candied angelica (see Cook's tip)
1 cup soft white bread crumbs
1 cup all-purpose flour, sifted
1 teaspoon baking powder

TOPPING
¼ cup butter, melted
⅓ cup sugar

1 Preheat the oven to 375°. Grease the base of an 8 inch round cake pan, then line with foil.

2 Make the topping: Mix the melted butter with the sugar and spread evenly over the base of the pan. Arrange the orange slices on top.

3 Beat the butter and sugar together until pale and fluffy, then beat in the orange rind. Add the eggs a little at a time, beating thoroughly after each addition. Fold in the cherries, angelica, bread crumbs, flour, baking powder and chopped orange flesh.

4 Turn the mixture into the prepared cake pan. Spread the mixture over the orange slices, then level the surface with a rubber spatula or the back of a large metal spoon. Bake 50-60 minutes, or until well risen and golden and the surface is just firm to the touch.

5 Leave the cake to cool 2-3 minutes. Run a small knife around the side of the cake, then turn out onto a warmed serving dish.

Cook's Notes

TIME
20 minutes preparation, 50-60 minutes baking.

PREPARATION
Finely grate the rind from the oranges and reserve. Peel the oranges with a sharp knife, taking care to remove every scrap of bitter white pith. Cut 8 well-shaped slices of orange, then chop the remaining orange flesh.

COOK'S TIP
If the angelica is dry and hard, soak in hot water for 5 minutes, drain and dry.

● 365 calories per portion

Peach flambé

SERVES 4

1 can (about 30 oz) peach halves
¼ cup brandy
¼ cup sweet butter
¼ cup sugar
⅓ cup medium-dry white wine
**1 tablespoon finely chopped
  shelled walnuts**

1 Drain the peaches well (see Cook's tip).
2 Pour the brandy into a cup and stand in a pan or bowl of hot water to warm through gently.
3 Melt the butter in a large, heavy-bottomed pan. Add the sugar and cook over low heat, stirring occasionally, until sugar has dissolved.

4 Stir in the wine, bring the mixture to a gentle simmer and add the peaches. Turn the peaches several times in the liquid to heat through and absorb the flavor. !
5 Remove the pan from the heat, pour the warmed brandy over the peaches and light. !
6 Allow the flames to die down, spoon into individual bowls and sprinkle with the walnuts. Serve at once.

Cook's Notes

 **TIME**
This special party dish takes just 15 minutes to prepare and serve.

! WATCHPOINTS
Turn the peaches gently with a wide spatula and a spoon so that they do not break up.
  When lighting the brandy, stand well back and hold the match just above the side of the pan.

SERVING IDEAS
Serve with whipped cream or ice cream and vanilla wafers or lady fingers.

 COOK'S TIP
The canned syrup is too sweet to be used in the flambé sauce. Put into a covered pitcher, it will keep 2-3 days. Use it as the liquid for poaching fresh fruit.

●400 calories per portion

Peach layer cake

MAKES 6 SLICES
3 eggs, separated
½ cup sugar
grated rind of ½ lemon
1 tablespoon lemon juice
⅓ cup fine semolina flour
3 tablespoons ground almonds
confectioners' sugar, for dusting
vegetable oil, for greasing

FILLING
¼ cup heavy cream
1 can (about 16 oz) peach slices,
well drained

1 Preheat the oven to 350°. Grease an 8 inch round layer cake pan. Line the base with waxed paper, then grease the paper.

2 In a large bowl, beat the egg yolks, sugar and lemon rind until thick and pale. Beat in the lemon juice, a little at a time. Stir in the semolina flour and almonds, then let stand for 10 minutes (see Cook's tips).

3 In a clean, dry bowl, beat the egg whites until standing in soft peaks. Using a large metal spoon, fold the egg whites into the semolina mixture (see Cook's tips).

4 Spoon the mixture into the prepared pan and bake in the oven for 30-40 minutes, until risen and golden and firm to the touch. Cool for 10 minutes, then turn out of the pan onto a wire rack. Peel off the lining paper and leave to cool.

5 To serve: Cut the cake in half horizontally with a long, serrated knife. Whip the cream until standing in soft peaks. Place 1 cake layer on a serving plate and spread with half the cream. Arrange the peaches over the cream. Place the remaining cake, cut side down, on top of the peaches and cream layer (see Cook's tips). Sift a little confectioners' sugar over the top of the cake to decorate and serve.

Cook's Notes

TIME
25 minutes preparation (including standing time), plus 30-40 minutes baking. Allow extra time for cooling and filling.

COOK'S TIPS
Leaving the mixture to stand softens the gritty texture of the semolina flour.

Do not overwork the mixture when adding the egg whites as this will make the cake heavy.

The cake can be filled up to 2 hours before serving and kept in the refrigerator.

VARIATION
Use 2 fresh peaches instead of canned fruit; peel, halve, pit and slice, then brush with lemon juice.

● 255 calories per slice

Peaches and bacon

SERVES 4
4 thick Canadian bacon slices (see Buying guide)
1 can (about 8 oz) peach slices, drained (see Economy)

SAUCE
¼ cup catsup
2 teaspoons Worcestershire sauce
1 tablespoon vinegar
1 tablespoon soft brown sugar
1 teaspoon vegetable oil
salt and freshly ground black pepper

FOR GARNISH
parsley sprigs
8 stuffed green olives

1 Line the broiler rack with foil. Preheat the broiler to moderate.

2 Make the sauce: In a bowl mix together the catsup, Worcestershire, vinegar, brown sugar, oil and salt and pepper to taste.

3 Arrange the bacon slices on the broiler rack. Spread half the sauce over them. Broil for 2-3 minutes.

4 Turn the bacon slices, arrange peach slices on each one, and sprinkle over the remaining sauce. Broil for 2-3 minutes.

5 Transfer to a warmed serving platter and serve at once, with the cooking juices poured over. Garnish with parsley sprigs and 2 olives speared on a wooden pick.

Cook's Notes

TIME
Preparation and cooking take about 20 minutes.

ECONOMY
Use the left-over strained peach juice in a fresh fruit salad.

BUYING GUIDE
Canadian bacon slices are available from most supermarkets.
Canned ham or smoked pork loin chops can be used instead; the chops may need 5-7 minutes cooking each side, in which case add the peach slices and more sauce 3-5 minutes before cooking is complete.

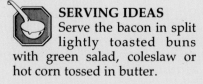

SERVING IDEAS
Serve the bacon in split lightly toasted buns with green salad, coleslaw or hot corn tossed in butter.

●275 calories per portion

Peaches in orange brandy

MAKES 3 × 1 PINT JARS
4 lb small peaches, peeled (see Buying guide)
1¼ cups water
finely grated rind and juice of 1 orange
½ cup sugar
1 cup brandy (see Economy)

1 Pour the water into a large, heavy-bottomed saucepan. Add the orange rind and juice and the sugar, then stir over low heat until the sugar has dissolved.
2 Halve and pit peaches. Add to the syrup, then cover and simmer gently until just heated through. ! Turn the fruit once during cooking so that it heats evenly. Using a slotted spoon, remove the peaches from the syrup and pack them into three 1 pint wide-mouthed sterilized canning jars. Stir the brandy into the remaining syrup, then pour this mixture over the peaches, leaving a ½ inch headspace at the top of each jar.
3 Meanwhile, pour 4-5 inches of water into a canner, with a rack in the bottom, and bring to a boil.
4 Put the closed jars on the rack in the canner so that they do not touch each other or the sides of the canner. Fill the canner with more boiling water to come 1-2 inches over the tops of the jars. Cover the canner and continue heating until the water comes to a rolling boil.
5 Process for 20 minutes, adjusting the heat under the canner so that the water stays at a gentle boil. ! Turn off the heat. Using tongs, lift the jars from the canner and put on a rack to cool. Leave undisturbed for 12 hours.
6 Label the jars, then store in a cool, dark place for 1 month before serving, to allow the flavor to mature and mellow (see Storage).

Cook's Notes

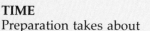

TIME
Preparation takes about 1 hour, but store for 1 month before serving.

WATCHPOINTS
Do not overcook the peaches or they will lose their shape.
It is important that the jars are completely covered with water during processing – top up with more boiling water if necessary.

BUYING GUIDE
Use small, slightly unripe, firm peaches. Larger ones can be used, but may need to be sliced before they are packed into the jars.

ECONOMY
The least expensive 3-star brandy is perfectly adequate, as the orange flavor in the syrup is strong.

STORAGE
Keep in a cool place. Use within 3 months.

SERVING IDEAS
Make this preserve while fresh peaches are in season: A jar will make a delicious gift.
Serve the peaches and syrup on their own, or with cream or ice cream; or include a few slices in fruit salads.

●270 calories per serving

Pear and beet salad

SERVES 4
2 medium pears
1 cup diced beets (see Cook's tips)
½ head fennel, trimmed and chopped (optional)
1 bunch watercress, stalks discarded

DRESSING
grated rind and juice of ½ lemon
1 tablespoon plain yogurt
1 tablespoon vegetable oil
1 teaspoon honey
½ teaspoon wine vinegar
salt and freshly ground black pepper

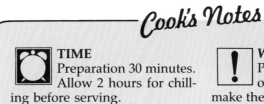

Cook's Notes

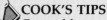

TIME
Preparation 30 minutes. Allow 2 hours for chilling before serving.

SERVING IDEAS
This salad goes very well with any cold meat or makes a colorful addition to an hors d'oeuvre tray.

VARIATIONS
If pears are not available, try substituting apples. Dairy sour cream may be used instead of yogurt. If you do not like the aniseed flavor of fennel, use celery, which has the same texture.

WATCHPOINT
Pears discolor quickly once they are peeled, so make the dressing first and dice the pears directly into it. The lemon juice will prevent them turning brown.

COOK'S TIPS
Canned beets are widely available and are suitable for this dish — drain them well before dicing.
Alternatively, you can buy ready-cooked beets from most supermarkets — peel them if the skin has been left on.

●100 calories per portion

1 First make the dressing: In a large bowl mix the lemon rind and juice with the yogurt, oil, honey and vinegar. Season with salt and pepper and beat with a fork until the ingredients are combined.

2 Peel, halve and core the pears, then dice and add to the dressing ⚠ with the beets and fennel, if using. Turn the mixture over gently to coat thoroughly.

3 Cover the salad with plastic wrap and refrigerate until needed. When ready to serve, tear the watercress leaves into small pieces and gently fold them into the salad. Pile the salad into a serving dish and serve at once.

Pear streusel

SERVES 4
4 firm ripe pears (see Buying guide)
¼ cup honey
finely grated rind and juice of 1 large lemon
butter, for greasing

TOPPING
¼ cup butter
2 cups soft white bread crumbs (see Cook's tips)
½ cup soft brown sugar
½ teaspoon apple pie spice

1 Preheat the oven to 375°. Butter a shallow, round flameproof dish which is just large enough to take 8 pear halves in a single layer.
2 Peel, halve and core the pears, then arrange cut side down in the prepared dish. Mix the honey with the lemon rind and juice, then spoon or pour over the pear halves.
3 Make the topping: Gently melt the butter, then remove from the heat and stir in the bread crumbs, sugar and spice, mixing well.

4 Sprinkle the topping evenly over the pears. Bake in the oven for about 45 minutes, or until the topping is golden brown and the pears are cooked (see Cook's tips). Serve the pears hot.

Cook's Notes

 TIME
Preparation and baking take about 1 hour.

BUYING GUIDE
Choose even-size dessert pears, such as Comice, Bartletts or Anjous for this recipe.

COOK'S TIPS
The bread crumbs should be dry, but soft; make them from a day-old loaf.
The exact cooking time depends upon the size and ripeness of the pears. Test them with a fine skewer: They should feel soft all the way through.

 SERVING IDEAS
Serve the dessert with whipping cream.
If you want to "stretch" to 8 servings, allow 1 pear half per person and top each portion with a generous scoop of vanilla ice cream.

 DID YOU KNOW
Streusel is the German word for crumble.

●320 calories per portion

Pear wine sherbet

SERVES 4
4 firm pears, peeled, cored and sliced (see Buying guide)
⅔ cup white wine (see Buying guide)
⅓ cup sugar
strip of lemon rind
maraschino cherries, to decorate

1 Put wine, sugar and rind in a saucepan and stir over low heat until the sugar has dissolved. Bring to a boil, add the pears, then cover the pan and poach the pears gently for about 5 minutes, or until tender. Remove the pan from the heat and set aside to cool.
2 Discard the lemon rind, reserve a few pear slices for decoration, then purée the cold mixture in a blender or press it through a strainer.
3 Pour into a freezer container, cover and freeze for several hours until firm (see Cook's tips).
4 Remove from the freezer and turn into a large bowl. [!] Break the sherbet up with a fork, then beat it well until slushy.
5 Spoon the mixture back into its freezer container, cover and return to the freezer for a further 3-4 hours until firm. [*]
6 Remove the sherbet from the freezer and allow it to soften at room temperature for about 15 minutes. Then spoon it into individual glasses and serve decorated with pear slices and maraschino cherries.

Cook's Notes

 TIME
Preparation takes only about 20 minutes, but remember to allow several hours for freezing time.

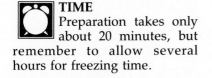 **FREEZING**
The sherbet can be stored in the freezer for up to 2 months.

 BUYING GUIDE
Choose firm dessert pears such as Comice for this sherbet.

It is worth choosing a good wine, or the flavor of the finished sherbet will be disappointing. Choose sweet or dry wine according to your own preference.

 WATCHPOINT
If the sherbet is too firm to mash, let it soften slightly at room temperature.

COOK'S TIPS
To make the sherbet in the freezing compartment of an ordinary refrigerator, use a pre-chilled shallow metal tray for freezing the sherbet and turn the refrigerator down to its coldest setting at least 1 hour before you start making the sherbet. This will speed up the freezing process.

 **VARIATION**
Decorate the sherbet with a few sprigs of fresh mint in season.

●140 calories per portion

Pears cooked in wine

SERVES 6
6 firm pears
2 cups white wine
¼ cup apricot preserves, strained
3 tablespoons soft brown sugar
¼ teaspoon ground cinnamon
2 whole cloves
thin strips of orange rind
juice of ½ lemon
3 tablespoons sliced almonds, toasted (optional)

1 Bring the wine, preserves, sugar and spices slowly to a boil in a deep saucepan.
2 Peel the pears, leaving them whole and with the stalks on. Immediately stand them upright in the saucepan, add the orange rind and lemon juice, cover tightly and simmer gently for 20-30 minutes or until just tender but not too soft (see Cook's tip).
3 Cut a thin slice from the bottom of each pear. Stand the pears upright in a serving dish. Boil the liquid in the uncovered saucepan for about 10 minutes to reduce by half. Strain and pour over the pears. Leave overnight to soak in the refrigerator or in a cool place. About 1 hour before serving, baste the pears well with the syrup.
4 Sprinkle the almonds over the pears just before serving.

Cook's Notes

TIME
Preparation and cooking take 40 minutes. Allow for soaking overnight.

COOK'S TIP
This is a good way of using hard pears. Cooking time will depend on the hardness of the fruit.

SERVING IDEAS
Serve with whipped cream and crisp cookies. Almond cookies go particularly well with pears.

PRESSURE COOKING
Cook the pears at high pressure for 1 minute.

VARIATIONS
Use red wine instead of white and substitute ¼ cup sugar for the preserves. To use canned pear halves instead of the fresh pears, boil the other ingredients together until the mixture is reduced by half, pour over the well-drained fruit and let soak.

●125 calories per portion

Pears in peanut sauce

SERVES 4
4 firm ripe pears (see Buying guide)
¼ cup sugar
grated rind and juice of ½ lemon
⅔ cup water
softened butter, for greasing

SAUCE
3 tablespoons smooth or crunchy peanut butter
2 tablespoons light soft brown sugar

1 Put the sugar, lemon rind and half the lemon juice into a heavy-bottomed saucepan. Stir in the water and heat gently, until the sugar has dissolved.
2 Meanwhile, core and peel the pears and brush immediately with the remaining lemon juice to pre-vent discoloration. Trim the bottom of each so it will stand upright.
3 Using a slotted spoon, lower the pears into the syrup. Brush a piece of waxed paper with butter and place over the pears, buttered side down. Cover the pan with a tight-fitting lid and poach gently until just tender (see Cook's tip). ⚠ Turn several times during cooking.

4 Remove the pan from the heat. Using a slotted spoon, transfer pears to a warmed serving dish.
5 Make the sauce: Measure syrup and make up to ⅔ cup, if necessary, with water. Put the peanut butter and brown sugar into a clean sauce-pan and gradually stir in the syrup. Stir over low heat until heated through; spoon over the pears.

Cook's Notes

TIME
10-15 minutes prepara-tion plus cooking time for the pears; the sauce takes about 5 minutes to make in total.

BUYING GUIDE
Choose nicely shaped pears of an even size so they cook in the same time. Dessert pears, such as Comice or Bartlett, are softer and sweeter than cooking varieties.

COOK'S TIP
Cooking time depends on the size, variety and ripeness of the pears. Allow about 20 minutes for dessert pears and up to 40 minutes for the cooking varieties. Use a fine skewer to test that they are tender.

 WATCHPOINT
Do not overcook, or the pears will disintegrate.

●220 calories per portion

Pineapple chicken

SERVES 4-6
3½ lb broiler/fryer, cut into 8
  serving pieces
½ cup all-purpose flour
salt and freshly ground black
  pepper
2 tablespoons butter or margarine
1 can (about 15 oz) pineapple rings
  in natural juice, drained, with
  juice reserved
2 tablespoons vegetable oil
1 large onion, thinly sliced
1¼ cups chicken broth
bouquet garni
¼ cup dairy sour cream

1 Preheat the oven to 350°.
2 Put the flour in a large plastic bag, season with salt and pepper, add half the chicken pieces and shake until well coated. Repeat with the remaining chicken pieces. Reserve the excess flour.
3 Melt the butter in a large skillet. Add the pineapple rings and cook over gentle heat, turning carefully with a spatula until golden brown on both sides. Remove, drain and set aside.

4 Heat the oil in the pan, then add the onion and cook for 5 minutes over gentle heat until soft and lightly colored. Push the onion to one side of the pan. Increase the heat slightly, add the chicken pieces to the pan; cook for about 5 minutes, turning until browned on all sides.
5 With a slotted spoon transfer the chicken pieces and onion to a large casserole. Add chicken broth to the pineapple juice to make up to 2 cups and add to the casserole with the bouquet garni and salt and pepper to taste.
6 Cover the casserole and cook in the oven for 30 minutes.
7 Remove from the oven and arrange the pineapple rings over the chicken in the casserole. Cover again and cook for a further 15 minutes or until the chicken is tender (the juices should run clear when the meat is pierced in the thickest part with a fine skewer). Reduce the oven temperature to 225°.
8 Arrange the chicken pieces and pineapple rings on a warmed serving platter and keep warm in the oven. Discard the bouquet garni and blot the excess fat from the surface of the cooking liquid with kitchen paper. Transfer the liquid to a pan and set over very low heat.

9 In a small bowl, mix 1 tablespoon of the reserved seasoned flour with the sour cream until smooth. Stir the mixture into the hot cooking liquid in the pan and beat until slightly thickened, but do not allow to boil. Taste and adjust seasoning. Spoon a little of the sauce over the chicken and pineapple and serve at once, with the remaining sauce passed separately.

Cook's Notes

TIME
Preparation, including pre-browning the chicken, takes about 20 minutes. Cooking in the oven and making the sauce take about 1 hour.

VARIATION
Use fresh pineapple, if available, instead of canned, but be sure to choose a large, ripe, sweet fruit. Slice off the top and bottom of the pineapple, thinly pare away the skin, cut into slices and remove the cores. Use 2 cups broth if using fresh pineapple.

●780 calories per portion

Pineapple creams

SERVES 4
1 can (about 8 oz) pineapple slices in natural juice, drained and chopped with juice reserved
about ¾ cup orange and passion fruit juice (see Buying guide)
1 envelope unflavored gelatin
3 eggs
¼ cup sugar
1 tablespoon drained preserved ginger, finely chopped
⅓ cup heavy cream

1 Make up the pineapple juice to 1¼ cups with orange and passion fruit juice. Put 3 tablespoons of the mixed juice into a heatproof bowl, sprinkle over the gelatin and leave to soak.
2 Meanwhile, separate 2 of the eggs.
3 Put the egg yolks, remaining egg and sugar into a large bowl. Using a table-top mixer (see Cook's tips), beat until the mixture is thick enough to retain the impression of the beaters for 3 seconds when the beaters are lifted.
4 Stand the bowl containing the gelatin in a pan of gently simmering water. Leave, stirring occasionally, for 1-2 minutes, until the gelatin is dissolved.
5 Beat the gelatin into the egg mixture, then beat in the mixed fruit juice. Leave in a cool place for about 15 minutes, until beginning to set (see Cook's tips).
6 Using clean beaters, beat the egg whites until standing in stiff peaks. Fold the egg whites into the gelatin mixture. Reserve some chopped pineapple for decoration and fold the rest into the egg mixture with the ginger.
7 Divide between 4 glass bowls, making sure the fruit is evenly distributed. Cover and refrigerate for 1 hour, or until set.
8 To serve: Beat the cream until it forms soft peaks, then pipe or spoon over each serving. Decorate each serving with the reserved pineapple and serve.

Pineapple crunch cream

SERVES 4

2 small pineapples
1¼ cups heavy cream
2 tablespoons confectioners' sugar, or to taste
¾ pint raspberries, well drained if frozen
1 tablespoon kirsch or light rum
½ cup peanut brittle

1 Prepare the pineapple shells (see Preparation). Cut the chunks of flesh into small pieces, discarding any tough, woody core. Place the pieces in a strainer set over a bowl and leave to drain.

2 Beat the cream with the sugar until it forms stiff peaks.

3 Reserve some raspberries for decoration. Lightly crush the remaining berries, then fold into the cream. Set aside some pineapple pieces, then fold the rest into the cream mixture with the kirsch. Turn the mixture into a plastic container, cover and refrigerate for 30 minutes or up to 4 hours.

4 Assemble the dessert: Fold half the crushed brittle into the cream mixture, then taste and add more sugar if liked. Spoon the mixture into the pineapple shells and decorate with the reserved pineapple and raspberries and crushed brittle. Serve at once. ⚠

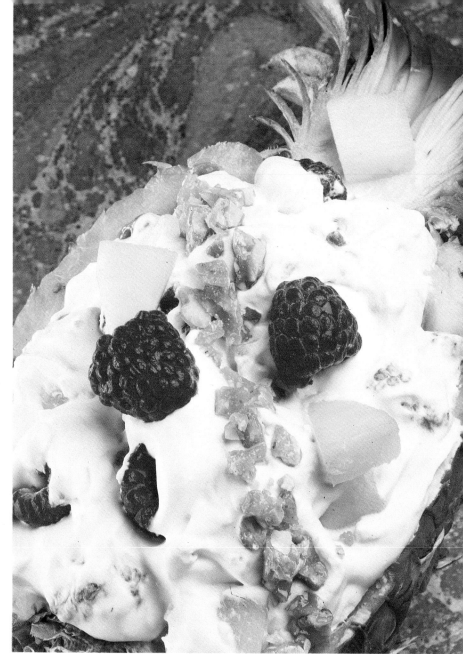

Cook's Notes

 TIME
Preparation takes about 1 hour. Allow extra time for chilling.

 WATCHPOINT
The crushed brittle will soften and melt if the dessert is left to stand.

 VARIATIONS
Use 1 large pineapple and serve the dessert piled into the shell of one half.
Strawberries can replace the raspberries.

● 560 calories per portion

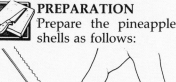 **PREPARATION**
Prepare the pineapple shells as follows:

1 *Cut each pineapple in half lengthwise, slicing through the leaves. Insert the blade of a long serrated knife into the flesh, about ¼ inch from the edge, at a 45° angle. Cut right around the inside.*

2 *Make 3 or 4 parallel cuts across the pineapple flesh and then 2-3 cuts lengthwise, taking care not to pierce the skin. Lift out the chunks of flesh with a teaspoon. Scrape out any excess flesh from the shells, then turn them upside-down and leave to drain.*

Pineapple meringue pie

MAKES 6 SLICES
2 cups graham cracker crumbs
6 tablespoons butter, melted

FILLING
2 tablespoons cornstarch
2 tablespoons sugar
1 can (about 16 oz) crushed
 pineapple, well drained, with
 syrup reserved
2 large eggs, separated (see
 Watchpoints)
1 cup sugar

1 Mix the crumbs with the melted butter. Spoon into a loose-bottomed 8 inch layer cake or flan pan and press evenly and firmly over bottom and up the side. Cover and refrigerate for at least 30 minutes.
2 Preheat the oven to 400°.

3 Make the filling: In a small, heavy-bottomed saucepan, mix together the cornstarch and sugar. Stir in a little of the reserved pineapple syrup to make a smooth paste, then blend in the remainder. Bring gently to a boil, stirring constantly, then remove from the heat.
4 Let mixture cool slightly, then beat in the egg yolks. Stir in the crushed pineapple. Spoon the pineapple mixture into the chilled shell and level the surface.
5 In a spotlessly clean bowl, beat the egg whites until they stand in stiff peaks. Beat in the sugar, 1 tablespoon at a time, and continue beating until the meringue is stiff and glossy.
6 Pipe swirls of meringue over pie or spread with a slim spatula, then draw up into peaks. Bake in the oven for 10-15 minutes, until the meringue is golden brown. Leave to cool completely, [!] then remove from the pan and place on a serving plate. Serve at room temperature.

Cook's Notes

TIME
30 minutes preparation, 10-15 minutes baking, plus at least 4 hours cooling.

WATCHPOINTS
Use eggs at room temperature.
Resist the temptation to remove the pie from the pan before it is completely cold as the pie shell may crumble.

STORAGE
The pie shell will keep for up to 2 days in the refrigerator. Wrap it well in foil or place in plastic bag and seal tightly. The baked pie will keep fresh overnight if left loosely covered in a cool place, but not the refrigerator.

●400 calories per slice

Pineapple sponge

MAKES 6-8 SLICES
¾ cup all-purpose flour
½ teaspoon apple pie spice
¼ teaspoon ground ginger
3 large eggs
6 tablespoons sugar
vegetable oil, for greasing

FILLING AND TOPPING
1 can (about 16 oz) crushed
    pineapple, drained with syrup
    reserved
3 tablespoons cornstarch
2 teaspoons lemon juice
a few drops yellow food coloring,
    (optional)
⅔ cup heavy whipping cream

1 Preheat the oven to 375°. Lightly grease two 7 inch layer cake pans, line the base of each with waxed paper, then grease the paper.
2 Sift the flour with the spices.

3 Put the eggs and sugar into a large heatproof bowl. Set the bowl over a pan half-full of gently simmering water. Using a rotary or hand-held electric beater, beat until the mixture will hold the trail of the beaters for 3 seconds when the beaters are lifted.
4 Remove the bowl from the pan and beat for a few minutes more until the mixture is cool. Using a large metal spoon, fold in the sifted flour one-third at a time.
5 Divide the mixture equally between the prepared pans and spread evenly by gently tilting the pans. Bake for 15 minutes until golden and springy to the touch.
6 Let stand for 2-3 seconds, then turn out onto a wire rack. Peel off the lining paper, turn the cakes right way up and leave until cold.
7 Meanwhile, make the filling: Make up the reserved pineapple syrup to 1¼ cups with water.
8 In a bowl, blend the cornstarch with some of the pineapple liquid. In a pan, bring the remaining liquid to a boil, then stir into the corn-

starch. Return to pan and simmer, stirring, until thickened.
9 Remove from the heat and stir in the crushed pineapple, lemon juice and yellow coloring, if using. Leave to cool completely.
10 Assemble the cake: Spread 1 sponge with two-thirds of the pineapple mixture. Place the remaining sponge on top and spread with the rest of the pineapple mixture, to within ½ inch of the edges. Whip the cream until standing in soft peaks, then pipe around the edge. (See Cook's tip). Serve at once.

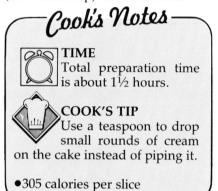

Cook's Notes

TIME
Total preparation time is about 1½ hours.

COOK'S TIP
Use a teaspoon to drop small rounds of cream on the cake instead of piping it.

● 305 calories per slice

Pineapple veal

SERVES 4

1½ lb stew veal, trimmed and cut
   into 1 inch cubes
1 tablespoon vegetable oil
1 onion, sliced
1 tablespoon all-purpose flour
1½-2 cups chicken broth
1 tablespoon vinegar
1 green pepper, seeded and thinly
   sliced
1 small fresh pineapple, pared,
   cored and cut into 1 inch chunks,
   or 1 can (about 8 oz) pineapple
   pieces, drained, with syrup
   reserved
½ cup sliced canned red
   pimientos
salt and freshly ground black pepper

1 Heat the oil in a large flameproof casserole. Add the onion and cook gently for about 5 minutes until soft.
2 Increase the heat slightly. Add the veal to the casserole, turn to coat in the oil and cook for about 5 minutes.
3 Sprinkle the flour into the casserole and stir well to mix.
4 If using fresh pineapple, stir in 2 cups chicken broth and the vinegar (or if using canned pineapple, stir in 1¼ cups broth, the vinegar and the syrup from the can). Bring to a boil, stirring, then lower the heat, cover and simmer the casserole for 1 hour.
5 Add the green pepper to the casserole and cook for a further 25 minutes.
6 Add the pineapple pieces and pimientos to the casserole. Season to taste with salt and pepper and cook for a further 15 minutes. Serve hot, straight from the casserole. ✳

Cook's Notes

TIME
Preparation, including pre-cooking, only takes about 20 minutes. Cooking then takes about 1 hour 40 minutes.

VARIATION
Boneless pork is a good alternative to veal.

FREEZING
Transfer to a rigid container, cool quickly, then seal, label and freeze for up to 6 months. To serve: Thaw in the refrigerator overnight, then heat through slowly on top of the stove until bubbling.

●265 calories per portion

Plum tartlets

MAKES 20
2 cups all-purpose flour
pinch of salt
½ cup butter or margarine
2 tablespoons sugar
water, to bind

FILLING
1½ tablespoons plum jam
10 large plums, halved and pitted
2 tablespoons soft brown sugar
⅔ cup heavy cream
2 squares (2 oz) semisweet
   chocolate (see Watchpoint)

1 Sift the flour and salt into a bowl. Cut the butter into ½ inch cubes, add to the flour and cut in until the mixture resembles fine crumbs. Add the sugar, mix lightly, then sprinkle in enough water to draw the mixture together into a firm dough.
2 Preheat the oven to 400°.
3 Turn the pastry onto a floured surface, knead lightly and roll out. Using a 3 inch fluted cookie cutter, cut out 20 circles and use to line deep tartlet pans (see Cook's tips). Prick the bases with a fork.
4 Spread about ¼ teaspoon jam over the base of each tartlet shell (see Cook's tips). Place half a plum in each shell, skin side up, and sprinkle with the sugar.
5 Bake in the oven, for 25-30 minutes or until the plums are just tender and the pastry is crisp and golden.
6 Remove from the oven, transfer the shells to a wire rack and leave until completely cold.
7 Whip the cream until it forms stiff peaks, then spoon or pipe a little on top of each plum. Grate the chocolate coarsely over the cream, then transfer the tarts to a large serving platter and serve.

Cook's Notes

TIME
30 minutes preparation, 25-30 minutes cooking, plus cooling time.

COOK'S TIPS
If you do not have enough tartlet pans, make the tartlets in batches. Leave the pastry, covered with plastic wrap, in the refrigerator in between baking batches.
   Use a stiff pastry brush for spreading the jam.

WATCHPOINT
If the weather is warm, chill the chocolate in the refrigerator for 30 minutes before grating or it may be too soft to grate satisfactorily.

VARIATION
When apricots are in season, use them instead of plums: replace the plum jam with apricot jam.

•140 calories per tartlet

Plums with pork

SERVES 4

8 thin boneless pork cutlets
1 can (about 20 oz) red plums
drained (see Buying guide)
2 tablespoons vegetable oil
2 tablespoons butter or
margarine
1 onion, finely chopped
⅔ cup dry white wine
1 teaspoon ground cinnamon
½ teaspoon ground coriander
salt and freshly ground black pepper

1 Carefully remove the pits from the plums, keeping them as whole as possible if using canned ones.
2 Make the sauce: Heat half the oil and half the butter in a pan, add the onion, cook gently for 10 minutes until softened. Pour in the wine and bring to a boil. Add the spices and salt and pepper to taste. Stir well, then lower the heat, cover and cook the sauce gently for 5 minutes, stirring occasionally.
3 Add the plums to the sauce, cover and simmer very gently for a further 5 minutes, taking care not to break up the plums. Taste and adjust seasoning.
4 Meanwhile, put the remaining oil and butter in a large skillet and heat gently. Add the pork cutlets and cook over high heat for 3 minutes on each side until the cutlets are cooked through and browned. ⚠
5 To serve: Arrange the cutlets on a warmed serving dish and spoon the sauce down the center of the cutlets. Serve at once.

Cook's Notes

TIME
This dish takes 35 minutes to prepare and cook.

WATCHPOINT
Do not overcook or keep the cutlets warm as they will toughen. They should be cooked while the sauce and plums are cooking.

BUYING GUIDE
If you use fresh plums you will need ½ lb pitted and sliced. Add them to the sauce with the wine and cook for 10-15 minutes.

●455 calories per portion

Prune pudding

SERVES 4
2 cups ready-soaked prunes
1¼ cups water
finely grated rind and juice of
 1 lemon
⅔ cup soft brown sugar
½ cup butter or margarine,
 softened
2 large eggs, lightly beaten
1½ cup fresh brown bread crumbs
¼ cup all-purpose flour, sifted
 with ¼ teaspoon baking powder
margarine or butter for greasing

1 Put the prunes into a heavy-bottomed saucepan with the water, half the lemon rind, the lemon juice and 2 tablespoons sugar. Cover and simmer gently until tender, then drain well and leave to cool.

2 Meanwhile, generously grease a 4 cup pudding mould.

3 Pit the prunes and use to line base and side of the greased mold to within ¾ inch of the rim. Beat the butter and the remaining sugar until pale and fluffy, then beat in the remaining lemon rind and the eggs. Stir in the brown bread crumbs and flour mixture.

4 Carefully spoon the egg mixture into the prepared mold. Cover the pudding with greased and pleated waxed paper or foil and secure in place with fine twine.

5 Place mold in a large, heavy-bottomed saucepan and pour in enough hot water to come halfway up side of mold. Cover pan with a well-fitting lid and steam pudding over low heat for 2 hours. Check water level during cooking and add boiling water, as necessary.

6 Protecting your hands with pot holders, lift mold out of pan. Let the pudding stand for 5 minutes, then remove covering and turn out. Serve at once.

Cook's Notes

 TIME
20 minutes cooking for the prunes, then 15 minutes preparation and 2 hours steaming time.

PRESSURE COOKING
Pour 5 cups boiling water into the bottom of the pressure cooker. Stand the mold on a trivet in cooker. Steam without pressure for 15 minutes, then bring to low (5 lb) pressure and cook for 30 minutes. Slowly reduce pressure. If using foil covering, add 10 minutes to the cooking time.

SERVING IDEAS
Serve the pudding hot, with a pitcher of chilled light cream.

●350 calories per portion

Prune tart

SERVES 4
2 cups ready-soaked prunes (see
  Buying guide)
⅔ cup red wine
¾ cup ground almonds
¼ cup sugar
½ egg white (approximately)
¼ cup currant jelly

PASTRY
1 cup all-purpose flour, sifted
  with pinch of salt
2 egg yolks
¼ cup sugar
¼ cup butter, diced

PASTRY CREAM
2 egg yolks
¼ cup sugar
1 tablespoon all-purpose flour
1 tablespoon cornstarch
1¼ cups milk
2-3 drops almond flavoring
¾ cup ground almonds
2 tablespoons heavy cream

1 Simmer the prunes in the red
wine for 5 minutes, then cool.
2 Meanwhile, make the pastry:
Beat the butter and sugar in a bowl
until light and fluffy. Beat in the egg
yolks, then stir in the flour and
knead until smooth. Place pastry

in a plastic bag and refrigerate for
30 minutes.
3 Preheat the oven to 375°.
4 Meanwhile, make the pastry
cream: Place the egg yolks in a bowl
with the sugar and flour and cornstarch and mix to a smooth cream
with a little milk.
5 Bring the remaining milk to just
below the boiling point, remove
from the heat and gradually stir into
the egg yolk mixture. Return to the
pan and beat constantly over low
heat until the mixture comes to a
boil.   Remove from the heat, stir
in a few drops of almond flavoring
to taste, then fold in the ground
almonds and cream. Leave the
custard to cool.
6 Place the chilled pastry in a lightly greased 8 inch flan pan or flan
ring placed on a baking sheet. Carefully press it out with your fingers
to line the pan evenly. Bake blind
for 15-20 minutes or until the pastry
is lightly browned. Leave the pastry
shell to cool.
7 Meanwhile, remove the prunes
from the wine with a slotted spoon,
reserving the wine, and pit them.
Mix the ground almonds with the
sugar and enough egg white to
form a paste. Stuff each prune with
almond paste and reshape.
8 When the flan shell is cool, carefully remove from the pan or ring
and place on a serving plate. Fill the
flan case with the pastry cream
(beating it first if a skin has formed)

and arrange the stuffed prunes in
circles on top.
9 Boil the reserved red wine for a
few minutes, until reduced to 3-4
tablespoons. Stir in the currant jelly
and melt over low heat, then boil
for 1-2 minutes until it forms a
glaze. Brush the prunes with the
glaze and leave to set. Serve at room
temperature.

Cook's Notes

TIME
Total preparation and
cooking time is 2 hours.
Add an extra 8½ hours for
soaking and cooking if not
using the ready-soaked prunes.

WATCHPOINTS
Be careful not to allow
the egg yolk mixture to
boil, or it may curdle.
   Take particular care to mold
the pastry evenly over the side
of the pan or flan ring.

BUYING GUIDE
Ready-soaked prunes,
now widely available
from supermarkets, are a great
time-saver for busy cooks. If
you use ordinary dried prunes,
remember that they may need
to be soaked before cooking.

●880 calories per portion

Raspberry favorite

SERVES 6

1½ pints fresh or frozen raspberries, thawed (see Variation)
1¼ cups heavy cream
3 tablespoons kirsch or medium sweet sherry
8 ready-made meringue shells (see Buying guide), roughly broken
½ cup confectioners' sugar, sifted
vegetable oil, for greasing

TO SERVE
12 fresh or frozen raspberries, thawed

1 Brush the inside of a 7 × 3 inch loaf pan with oil and place in the bottom of the refrigerator. Leave to chill for about 1 hour.
2 Whip the cream until it forms soft peaks, then add the kirsch and whip again until it has thickened.
3 Fold in the meringue pieces with a metal spoon and add 1 tablespoon of the sugar.
4 Turn the mixture into the chilled pan, cover with foil, seal, label and freeze.
5 Prepare the raspberry sauce: Press the raspberries through a strainer into a bowl, or work in a blender. Stir in the confectioners' sugar and mix well. Pour into a rigid container, seal, label and freeze.
6 To serve: Thaw the raspberry sauce for 2-4 hours at room temperature. Just before serving, remove the ice cream from the freezer and remove wrappings. Dip the base of the pan into hot water for 1-2 seconds, then invert a serving platter on top. Quickly invert the pan onto the platter, giving a sharp shake halfway around. Pour a little of the sauce over the mold, decorate with raspberries and serve at once. Pour the remaining sauce into a pitcher and pass separately.

Cook's Notes

TIME
Total preparation time, including chilling the pan, is 1½ hours. (Can be kept in the freezer for up to 3 months.) After freezing, allow 2-4 hours to thaw the raspberry sauce at room temperature before serving.

BUYING GUIDE
Packages of meringue shells or nests are readily available in most good supermarkets and many delicatessens.

VARIATION
Any summer fruit can be used for this ice cream, such as strawberries, currants, blueberries or blackberries.

●380 calories per portion

Red currant and port lamb

SERVES 4

16 very thin lamb chops
salt and freshly ground black
 pepper
3 tablespoons butter or margarine
2 tablespoons vegetable oil
1 red pepper, seeded and finely
 sliced
1 tablespoon wholewheat flour
1 tablespoon Worcestershire sauce
1¼ cups chicken broth
¼ cup port
¼ cup red currant jelly (see
 Economy)
½ lb small mushrooms
1 tablespoon chopped fresh
 parsley

1 Season the chops with salt and pepper. Melt 1 tablespoon of the butter in the oil in a large skillet. Add the chops and cook over moderate heat for 5-7 minutes, turning once to brown on both sides. Lower the heat and cook for 2 minutes more on each side. Remove the chops from the pan, arrange them on a warmed serving dish and keep hot.

2 Add the red pepper to the pan and cook gently for 5 minutes, until softened. Remove the pepper from the pan with a slotted spoon and sprinkle over the lamb chops.

3 Sprinkle the flour into the skillet and cook, stirring, for 1-2 minutes. Gradually stir in the Worcestershire, broth, port and red currant jelly. Bring to a boil, stirring, then lower the heat and simmer very gently until the red currant jelly has melted. Taste and adjust seasoning if necessary.

4 Meanwhile, melt the remaining butter in a small saucepan. Add the mushrooms and cook gently for about 5 minutes.

5 Strain the hot sauce over the lamb chops and pepper, and arrange the cooked mushrooms around the edge of the dish. Sprinkle with the parsley and serve at once.

Cook's Notes

TIME
This dish takes 20-30 minutes to prepare and cook.

ECONOMY
Use red currant jelly containing port, which is available from delicatessens: although this is more expensive than ordinary red currant jelly, it is less expensive than buying port specially for the recipe.

DID YOU KNOW
Port is fortified wine — that is it is mixed with brandy while still containing at least half of its grape sugar. The brandy stops fermentation, and the result is a wine that is sweet and strong. Traditionally port is made from grapes grown in the upper Douro valley of Portugal.

●765 calories per portion

Rhubarb and orange cream

SERVES 4
1 can (about 20 oz) rhubarb
finely grated rind and juice of 1 orange
1 tablespoon sugar, or to taste
3 eggs
⅔ cup heavy cream
cookies, to serve

1 Put the rhubarb and 2 tablespoons juice from the can into a blender with the orange rind and juice and sugar. Blend at high speed until the mixture forms a smooth purée.

2 Beat the eggs together thoroughly in a heatproof bowl, then beat in the rhubarb purée.

3 Place the bowl over a saucepan of simmering water and cook for 10-15 minutes, beating constantly with a wire whisk until the mixture is thick and creamy. !

4 Remove the bowl from the heat, leave to cool, then chill in the refrigerator until absolutely cold. !

5 Whip the cream until it stands in soft peaks, then fold into the cooled rhubarb mixture. Cover and chill in the refrigerator for at least 6 hours (preferably overnight) before serving.

6 Divide the chilled cream between 4 individual dishes or glasses and serve at once with cookies.

Cook's Notes

TIME
1 hour 25 minutes, plus at least 6 hours chilling.

VARIATIONS
Use fresh rhubarb when in season. Trim and slice 1 lb rhubarb, then cook with sugar to taste until tender. Drain, reserving 2 tablespoons juice.

Try using canned pitted plums instead of rhubarb, but strain them after puréeing to remove the skins. Add a pinch of ground cinnamon to give a deliciously different flavor.

COOK'S TIPS
If you do not have a blender, simply mash the rhubarb thoroughly until it is a smooth, creamy pulp.

Use the finest part of the grater to grate the orange rind. Do not grate for too long in one place, but simply take off the rind, or the orange-colored part of the skin, because the pith underneath is rather bitter.

WATCHPOINTS
It is important the bowl containing the eggs and rhubarb purée should not come in contact with the water simmering in the pan. It should rest above the surface of the water so the mixture does not boil and curdle and separate.

The cooked mixture must be chilled before you add the cream, or the cream will flop.

SERVING IDEAS
This dessert has a soft, creamy consistency which is complemented by crisp cookies such as *langues de chat* or lady fingers.

●250 calories per portion

Rhubarb roulade

MAKES 5 SLICES
1½ lb rhubarb, chopped
½ cup sugar
3 tablespoons water
5 large eggs, separated
⅔ cup all-purpose flour, sifted
with a pinch of baking powder
¼ cup sugar
few drops red food coloring
confectioners' sugar, for dredging
vegetable oil, for greasing
cream, to serve

FILLING
1 dessert apple
finely grated rind and juice of
½ lemon
1 cup cottage cheese, strained
2 tablespoons sugar, or to taste

1 Put chopped rhubarb into an enameled pan with the sugar and the water. Cover and simmer until tender, then remove from heat and cool completely.
2 Preheat the oven to 375°. Grease a 10½ × 15½ × 1 inch jelly roll pan, then line the base of the pan with waxed paper.
3 Drain the rhubarb, then put it into a large bowl with the egg yolks and mix with a fork until blended. Stir in the flour mixture, sugar and red food coloring and mix well.
4 In a clean dry bowl, beat the egg whites until standing in stiff peaks. Using a metal spoon, fold the egg whites into the rhubarb mixture. Pour the mixture into the prepared pan and immediately bake in the oven for 20-25 minutes, until springy to the touch.
5 Meanwhile, prepare the filling: Core, but do not pare the apple, then coarsely grate it. Put the grated apple into the bowl and thoroughly stir in the lemon rind and juice.
6 Lay a large sheet of waxed paper on top of a clean, damp dish towel. Sprinkle paper evenly with confectioners' sugar.
7 Cool the rhubarb sponge in the pan for 10 minutes, then run a round-bladed knife around the side to loosen it and turn out onto the sugared waxed paper.
8 Drain the apple and mix with the strained cheese and sugar, to taste. Spread the mixture over the rhubarb sponge. Roll up the sponge from one short end, with the aid of the paper. Press the join. Carefully transfer rhubarb roll to a serving plate, placing it seam-side down. Sift confectioners' sugar over the top and serve at once.

TIME
Total preparation time is about 1¼ hours.

WATCHPOINT
The sponge will become soggy if left to stand: serve it as soon as it is ready, cutting it into neat slices with a sharp serrated knife.

DID YOU KNOW
Roulade is the French word for roll.

●255 calories per slice

Rhubarb tipsy

SERVES 6

**1 lb rhubarb, cut into 1 inch lengths
(see Cook's tips)**
**¾ cup butter or margarine,
softened**
¾ cup light soft brown sugar
1 tablespoon light corn syrup
½ teaspoon ground ginger
2 eggs, lightly beaten
**1½ cups all-purpose flour, sifted
with 2 teaspoons baking powder**
**1-2 tablespoons dark rum or milk
margarine or butter, for greasing**

1 Preheat the oven to 350°. Grease a
9 inch round layer cake pan (see
Cook's tips).
2 Beat the butter and sugar
together until pale and fluffy. Stir
the syrup into one-third of the
mixture, then spread this evenly
over the base of the prepared pan.
3 Arrange the rhubarb over the top,
in circles radiating out from the
center of the pan. Cover as much of
the syrup mixture as possible with
the fruit, trimming the pieces to fit if
necessary. Sprinkle the ginger over
the rhubarb, then set aside.
4 Beat the eggs a little at a time into
the remaining butter mixture,
adding 1 tablespoon of the flour
mixture with the last few additions
of egg. Using a large metal spoon,
fold in the remaining flour mixture,
then stir in sufficient rum or milk to
give the mixture a soft dropping
consistency (see Cook's tips).
5 Spoon the mixture into the pan
and spread it evenly over the rhubarb. Bake in the oven for about 45

minutes, until the sponge top is
well risen and the pudding is
springy to the touch at the center.
6 Cool the pudding for 2-3 minutes,
then run a round-bladed knife
around edge to loosen it. Turn out
onto a serving dish and serve
warm.

Cook's Notes

 TIME
25 minutes preparation
and 45 minutes baking.

COOK'S TIPS
Cut the rhubarb into
equal pieces, slicing any
large chunks in half, so that it
will cook evenly.
  A French sponge tin (*moule à
manqué*) is ideal for this recipe:
its sloping sides give the
turned-out pudding an attractive shape. If you do not have
one use a 9 inch layer cake pan
which is 2 inches deep.
  To test the consistency, scoop
up some of the mixture on a
rubber spatula; hold the spatula
on its side just above the bowl
and tap the handle gently and
once only against the rim; the
mixture should drop easily into
the bowl.

 **SERVING IDEAS**
Serve the pudding
warm, with light cream,
or let cool completely and serve
as a cake.

VARIATION
Use orange rind instead
of the ginger and Coin-
treau in place of rum.

●475 calories per portion

Strawberry charlotte russe

SERVES 6
1 package strawberry-flavored
   gelatin
1 cup boiling water
about 20 lady fingers
1 envelope whipped dessert
   topping mix
1 cup cold milk
vegetable oil, for greasing

TO DECORATE
a few fresh strawberries, sliced
½ cup heavy cream
   (optional)

1 Rinse the base of a 6 inch charlotte mold with cold water, pouring off any excess (see Did you know). Brush the inside of the rim lightly with oil (see Cook's tip). Set the mold aside.

2 Sprinkle the gelatin over the boiling water and stir until it has dissolved. Measure the gelatin mixture and make up the quantity to 1¾ cups with cold water.

3 Spoon or pour ½ a cup of the gelatin mixture onto the base of the mold and refrigerate for about 15 minutes or until set. Refrigerate the remaining gelatin mixture separately for about 45 minutes, until it has thickened to a syrupy consistency.

4 Line the sides of the mold with the lady fingers, placing the tapered end at the bottom of the mold (see Preparation).

5 Sprinkle the dessert mix over the milk and beat until thickened and standing in peaks. Beat in the syrupy gelatin, then spoon into the mold and level the surface. Refrigerate for about 1 hour or until firm and set. [!]

6 With a sharp knife, trim the lady fingers level with the filling. Dip the bottom of the mold in a bowl of hot water for 1-2 seconds, then invert a serving plate on top. Invert the mold onto the plate and turn the charlotte russe out.

7 Decorate the charlotte russe with sliced strawberries and whipped cream, if liked. Serve immediately or cover loosely and refrigerate for up to 2 hours.

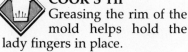

Cook's Notes

TIME
20 minutes preparation, plus several hours chilling time.

SERVING IDEAS
For an attractive finish, try tying a wide ribbon around the charlotte when it is unmolded — this is a particularly good way of supporting the sides, if you have used a softer variety of lady fingers.

DID YOU KNOW
Metal charlotte molds are specially designed for molded desserts which are turned out for serving. (The size is the diameter of the top of the mold, not the bottom.) If you do not have one, use a 4 cup soufflé mold instead.

COOK'S TIP
Greasing the rim of the mold helps hold the lady fingers in place.

PREPARATION
Trim the sides of the lady fingers straight, if necessary. If using a charlotte mold, slice one end off each finger so that it tapers slightly.

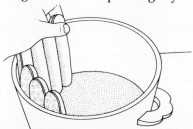

Stand the lady fingers upright, with the sugared surface against the side. Place them as close together as possible to prevent the filling seeping out.

WATCHPOINT
Do not attempt to turn out the dessert until the filling is very firm and set, or it will collapse.

●195 calories per portion

INDEX